Open to Change
Options for Teaching
Self-Directed Learners

OTHER GOODYEAR BOOKS IN GENERAL METHODS & CENTERS

AH HAH! The Inquiry Process of Generating and Testing Knowledge, John McCollum

A CALENDAR OF HOME/SCHOOL ACTIVITIES, Jo Anne Patricia Brosnahan and Barbara Walters Milne

CHANGE FOR CHILDREN Ideas and Activities for Individualizing Learning, Sandra N. Kaplan, Jo Ann B. Kaplan, Sheila K. Madsen, Bette K. Taylor

CREATING A LEARNING ENVIRONMENT A Learning Center Handbook, Ethel Breyfogle, Susan Nelson, Carol Pitts, Pamela Santich

THE LEARNING CENTER BOOK An Integrated Approach, Tom Davidson, Phyllis Fountain, Rachel Grogan, Verl Short, Judy Steely, Katherine Freeman

ONE AT A TIME ALL AT ONCE The Creative Teacher's Guide to Individualized Instruction Without Anarchy, Jack E. Blackburn and W. Conrad Powell

OPEN SESAME A Primer in Open Education, Evelyn M. Carswell and Darrell L. Roubinek

THE OTHER SIDE OF THE REPORT CARD A How-to-Do-It Program for Affective Education, Larry Chase

THE TEACHER'S CHOICE, Sandra N. Kaplan, Sheila K. Madsen, Bette T. Gould

TEACHING FOR LEARNING Applying Educational Psychology in the Classroom, Myron H. Dembo

OTHER WAYS, OTHER MEANS Altered Awareness Activities for Receptive Learning, Alton Harrison and Diann Musial

WILL THE REAL TEACHER PLEASE STAND UP? A Primer in Humanistic Education, second edition, Mary Greer and Bonnie Rubinstein

A YOUNG CHILD EXPERIENCES Activities for Teaching and Learning, Sandra N. Kaplan, Jo Ann B. Kaplan, Sheila K. Madsen, Bette T. Gould

For information about these, or Goodyear books in Language Arts, Reading, Science, Math, and Social Studies, write to

Janet Jackson
Goodyear Publishing Company
1640 Fifth Street
Santa Monica, Calif. 90401
(213) 393-6731

HAL D. MALEHORN developed open concepts with primary grades children for 15 years before becoming associate professor of elementary education at Eastern Illinois University. He has developed courses and workshops on open education and is the author of ENCYCLOPEDIA OF TEACHING ACTIVITIES FOR GRADES K-3 and a contributing editor for DAY CARE AND EARLY EDUCATION.

Open to Change
Options for Teaching
Self-Directed Learners

Hal Malehorn, Ph.D.
Eastern Illinois University

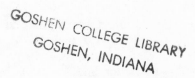

Goodyear Publishing Company • **Santa Monica, California**

Library of Congress Cataloging in Publication Data

Malehorn, Hal, 1930-
Open to change.

    Bibliography: p.
    1. Open plan schools. I. Title.
LB 1029.06M34   371.3   77-28653
ISBN 0-87620-626-7
ISBN 0-87620-625-9 pbk.

Y-6267-2 (C)
Y-6259-9 (P)

Current printing (last digit):
10 9 8 7 6 5 4 3 2 1

Design and Art: Linda M. Robertson

Printed in the United States of America

contents

prologue

Several special features make *Open to Change, Options for Teaching Self-Directed Learners* a uniquely helpful book. First, it presents a novel point of view. In defining my theoretical orientation, I not only enumerate and describe the eight essential principles of openness, but I also distinguish between these cardinal tenets and the five optional conditions that are frequently associated with open classrooms, detailing how both these principles and circumstances are best interpreted in daily interaction with children. In addition, the historical beginnings of the open movement in British primary education are traced, and response is made to nine false notions that have lately arisen concerning the application of open techniques in American schools.

Secondly, this book is both thorough and complete. In preparing materials, I have consulted several hundred articles, research reports, documents, and books dealing with all the different elements of openness, and have distilled and simplified the best expert opinion on this timely topic to present a clear and definitive statement explaining what national open education might become. *Open to Change, Options for Teaching Self-Directed Learners* treats every important part of this subject, including a discussion of how to assess pupil progress, how to build self-discipline among students, and how to procure professional resources.

A final feature of this book is its practicality. To complement the personal point of view presented in the first section of the work, useful suggestions are offered in the second, and longer, section. Worth special note are the more than 350 labeled and check-marked ideas, each one a useful hint explaining a workable technique in such areas as changing the curriculum to suit open goals, developing learning centers in classrooms, and managing the dozens of daily details that are inevitable in self-directed instructional situations. This book also presents a step-by-step outline showing the teacher how to open her style one element at a time, in keeping with her time, her organizational skills, and the ability of her students to handle the responsibilities that are a part of open classrooms. To amplify further the techniques suggested in the book, fifty-three illustrative figures—such as questionnaires and surveys, pupil contracts, all-purpose self-checking aids, learning center diagrams, charts, graphs, and other assessment devices—are included. In addition, the book contains a list of useful discards and low-cost materials, and an annotated bibliography summarizing nineteen major works that deal with related aspects of open education.

Open to Change, Options for Teaching Self-Directed Learners is mainly for teachers because good teaching has always been the key to the success of any instructional program. Teachers invest their days in planning, arranging, changing, coping, struggling, inventing, and relating. Without an effective adult in the classroom, students are unable to fulfill the measure of promise they bring with them when they enter school. In the open classrooms, where pupils assume major responsibilities for their own educational growth, the role of the teacher is even more important than it is in more traditional settings.

This book is also for others: for administrators who provide both the knowledgeable support and the physical facilities that allow open learning to happen; for parents who want to know what goes on in a good open classroom; and for boards of education and other members of the community, who deserve to have an institution that serves their children well.

In keeping with the very nature of openness, the many suggestions included in this book are presented as alternatives that are appropriate to many different situations. Although the open movement began some years ago in British primary schools, the fundamentals of openness are as useful in junior high school, high school, and university classrooms as they are in elementary classrooms. With a modest amount of imagination any teacher should be able to adapt the ideas presented in this work to any grade level in virtually any type of situation. Since this book develops many more ideas than could ever be utilized in any single setting, the teacher is invited to select only those items that best meet her* instructional goals. If any reader can take any single major concept or method proposed in this work and make it operate successfully in a single classroom or throughout a school system, this book will have been worthwhile.

Hal Malehorn

* Only as a matter of consistency and convenience, throughout the text of this book the pronoun "she" refers to the typical teacher, while "he" is used to designate both the classroom student and the school principal. No social comment concerning the appropriateness of such labels is intended.

part one
Defining Open Education

chapter one
The Essential Principles of Openness

Taking a Look at Terms

Finding an adequate definition for open education has been a challenge for nearly a decade. Since 1967 when Joseph Featherstone wrote a series of landmark articles detailing dramatic techniques he had just observed in British schools, professionals in America have struggled with the problem of defining openness in ways that would permit this new concept to fit within the framework of American pedagogy. This search for comprehensive statements has not been easy.

One difficulty in defining openness is inherent in the very process of labeling. Open education involves human beings and concepts, and neither have ever been simple to classify. "Open education" is a term somewhat like "democracy," "freedom," and "self-government," all of which have defied adequate interpretation for centuries. Furthermore, open education does not lend itself well to analysis because the concept of openness is always in the process of becoming, but is never finished; there is always something more to discover, and the search for more effective ways of teaching is almost as important as the definition itself. Similarly, open approaches are highly personalized. Open techniques stress flexible use of materials, media, and space, as well as variability and individuality in learning activities. In this sense open education for one teacher may well involve circumstances and methods that are not useful for another.

Many different terms have appeared lately in the professional literature dealing with open education. Some of these have been used as equivalent labels for openness, while others describe important elements of this new approach:

open access	open day
open area	open schedule
open choice	open school
open classroom	open space
open corridor	open structure
open curriculum	open university

Other expressions in the books, periodicals, and research reports reflect contemporary British practices that have profoundly influenced the open movement:

British Infant Schools	integrated day
Leicestershire model	integrated curriculum
family plan	unscheduled day
vertical grouping	

Still other labels are variations on the main theme, or they suggest historical antecedents for present open interests:

life adjustment learning	individual progress
activity center learning	continuous progress
alternative education	schools without walls
personalized learning	new schools
informal education	free schools
child-centered approach	

Regardless of the multiplicity of definitions, it is important to remember that neither labels nor organizational schemes guarantee good teaching—rather, only people can make openness work. For all the variations in programs and terminology, nothing will succeed unless teachers and principals and parents and children labor together in pursuit of enlightenment. The real challenge is to take at least one important idea and see how well it can be implemented in the daily lives of children in school.

However difficult it may be to define open education, a study of the professional literature on the subject reveals a recurring set of characteristics that tend to be found in most open classrooms. Individual authors, of course, describe these concepts in different ways with different emphases. Although not all these conditions of openness are equally important to every expert in the field, there does seem to be considerable agreement on at least eight important principles.

The Need for Self-Directed Learning

The first consensual principle of openness is self-direction; the focus of open education is clearly on the individual child, and the learner himself is deeply involved in planning his own course of study. Self-direction is set in motion by the child's own motivations. The best learning springs from the child's own enthusiasm and his own interests, rather than from an adult's arbitrary and sometimes artificial interjections of purpose and meaning for each instructional activity. In the traditional classroom an essential part of the teacher's planning includes her answer to the question "How can I get children interested in *my* lesson?" Her motivating device frequently takes the form of some question or demonstration that is intended to capture her pupils' attention long enough for her to show the relationship between the motivating element and the lesson at hand. In contrast, the teacher in the open classroom seizes upon interests that the children already have. The students themselves are encouraged to take the initiative in finding meaning in learning, topics to pursue, media to utilize, and needs to satisfy. The open teacher discovers these interests through inventories, autobiographies, personal diaries, and casual conversation. She responds also to interesting situations that arise; for example, she quickly capitalizes on the learning potential of the first hard spring rain, the bulldozer at work in the next-door lot, and the birds and animals that unexpectedly visit the playground. There are in truth very few interests that cannot somehow be used to motivate individual learning in the open classroom.

Another important element of self-directed learning is self-pacing. The open teacher is aware that no two children learn at the same rate, even on those infrequent occasions when they are using the same learning materials. Children studying in open settings are permitted to proceed through materials at individual speeds at which they are most comfortable and which are consistent with their specific abilities. Self-pacing does not imply that all children must be made to study at maximum speed or to hurry through a set of activities, because there are very few people who are capable of studying at top efficiency for long periods. Rather, children should be encouraged to vary the intensity of their learning, shifting from relatively easy work to more demanding tasks in a way that guarantees a general rate of progress with which they can be satisfied. Furthermore, since learning is not always vertical, each self-paced pupil is encouraged to explore the by-paths of learning as well as the principal routes. His progress through a set of materials may be as often horizontal and enriching as it is vertical and complex.

A third part of self-orientation is self-selection. The goal of the open teacher is to transfer to the learner as much responsibility for learning as he is capable of handling. In the ideal application of this concept the child is able to choose which subjects he is to study, which learning materials are most appropriate to his instructional objectives, what amount of time he is to spend on each activity, and how fast he should work to complete each task. Really, however, there are few students with the background and the maturity to take such complete charge of their learning. In fact, most students in American schools probably find it more comfortable to cluster about their teacher and to ask "What do you want me to do now?" Self-selection, therefore, becomes a matter of degree; the teacher identifies the extent to which each student can manage the different choices, and she gives added training and practice to those pupils who find decision making difficult to master. If the open classroom includes many children with limited experience or with limited initiative, the instructor needs to suggest learning possibilities by presenting a wide range of interesting and useful activities.

Self-assessment is a fourth element of self-directed learning. In the open classroom the child has a major share in appraising his progress and in maintaining his personal records of accomplishment. No longer is the teacher entirely responsible for correcting students' answers. No longer does she alone report pupil progress to the parents of her children. The student is involved daily in evaluating his success: he sometimes uses programmed materials that immediately show him how well he has mastered a concept or a skill, he checks his own papers using the teacher's answer sheets, and he keeps a chart or a graph which shows visually his success with spelling or mathematics. Tests are administered at his own request when he feels confident he can attain a predetermined degree of competency. The child discusses his progress with the teacher in private conferences and maintains a diary summarizing his impressions about himself, his peers, and his school. He is often a member of a three-way conference including his parents, his teacher, and himself.

Making Instruction Relevant

Relevance is an essential principle in open education because it suggests that learning must be related to the child and to his personal world. In practice, relevance is demonstrated when experiences occurring outside the school are brought into the classroom. Relevance is also present as the child learns to apply his classroom learning to his roles as a member of a family and a citizen in the community. Further, learning is most effective when it relates directly to the immediacy of each moment. Children at all ages find it hard to learn something that might be useful to them someday but has no immediate value. The open teacher shows the relationship of learning to situational needs. For example, the child's mastery of arithmetic serves him when he takes a trip to a local store, the meaning of environmental concern is translated into cleaning up a littered lot or in reusing discarded materials in the classroom, and mastery of spelling is essential in composing a letter to a relative or a friend.

In addition to relating learning to immediate real-life needs, the open teacher shows important relationships between different subject areas. In the traditional school the child shifts his attention from one subject to another, often moving from room to room in response to bells indicating allocated times and schedules invented by adults. The typical student may have as many as six or eight specialists teaching him at different times of the day. In contrast, the open teacher makes a special effort to show her children the close ties between art and music, and the interdependence of science and mathematics. She often has a greater opportunity to combine short periods into one longer period. She may be better able to ignore the tyranny of bells, to permit her pupils to intermingle a variety of topics drawn from many different subject areas. On some days the need to pursue children's natural interests may take priority over the need to cover material in a textbook. Then too, the open teacher uses a greater variety of materials to permit more contact between different areas of study. For example, she may use the social studies textbook to develop reading skills, she may introduce arithmetic skills in science class to help children perform an experiment more accurately, or she may explore movement in music and art to give her students a sense of rhythm.

The open teacher also develops the child's understanding of the relationship between his school, his home, and his community. The locus of learning is no longer the classroom alone, but the entire school building, the playground, and the surrounding neighborhood help the child to apply knowledge to new situations and provide new instructional opportunities. The open teacher identifies members of the community who can serve as resource persons for her children. The home becomes an extension of the school. The term "homework" changes its meaning, for no longer is it a burdensome chore assigned equally to all children and completed only after parental nagging. Rather, the students' work-at-home includes experiences that are both meaningful and interesting. These activities are unique to each child selecting them and may reflect a hobby or some other special interest or aptitude. If specific skills need to be practiced at home, the child decides where, when, and how he will do so. When it is feasible, such "homework" may involve other members of the family in trips to a museum or in musical, artistic, or photographic expression. Awareness of relevance is also present when parents attend their children's in-school classes either as visitors or as volunteers. Informal activities may attract the children and their families back to school in the late afternoons or the early evenings.

Enhancing Uniqueness

Another major principle of the open classroom is an awareness of the unique nature of each person in it. Variability is noticed, respected, and cherished. Not only does the open teacher help the children identify the more obvious differences among children—such as variations in appearance, height, weight, and choice of clothing—but she also helps her young charges to see the importance of the more subtle differences in beliefs, styles of living, interests, and capabilities. The open teacher encourages her children to think in divergent ways. No longer is the teacher seen as an authority figure; no longer does she expect each child's ideas to conform to her own. Instead, students are encouraged to go well beyond the teacher's thinking, to identify many different ways of solving problems, to discover completely new sources of information, to question data that are not correct, to seek out justifications for answers, to pursue the unexpected and unusual topic, and to differ freely from the teacher when disagreement is appropriate. Better ways, newer facts, and more compelling logic are all respected, regardless of the source. And if a child occasionally excels his teacher, she offers full credit and praise.

By applying the notion of uniqueness to the curriculum, the teacher helps each child to identify and to develop every talent at his command. Particularly in creative endeavors such as art, music, dance, poetry, dramatics, and storytelling, the teacher allows the child to express himself in natural and non-prescriptive ways. She stresses each child's efforts, insight, and inventiveness, and avoids stereotyping children's thinking through conformist comments such as "Look at Steven's painting, boys and girls. Isn't he doing a *beautiful* job?" or "Listen to this music, children, and then Janet will show us how an elephant should move." In addition, the teacher gives as much credit to talents that do not fit neatly into the curriculum as she gives to those talents that do. The child who has a gift for inventing new mechanical devices need not wait until a high school shop class capitalizes on his skill. The student who knows how to spin a top can demonstrate this ability as a part of a general physical training session in which some of his peers are encouraged to learn it too.

Encouraging Exploration

Closely related to uniqueness and creativity is the open teacher's emphasis on experimentation and exploration. Particularly at the early grade levels, the open classroom provides many concrete items for the child to manipulate because the physical handling of learning objects must precede the formation of generalizations about them. When he is developing number skills, for example, the child handles a set of acorns or bottle caps as he counts them or as he multiplies subsets. Eventually he learns the number facts that he has demonstrated firsthand. In art class the child investigates the mixing of pigments as he mingles paints on paper. This helps him see the relationship between primary and secondary colors much more clearly than would the traditional color wheel. Of course, science offers still other possibilities for examination and discovery; the teacher poses questions and problems, and the child frames his reasoned guesses, then compares the outcome of an experiment with his anticipated results. In movement exploration, the child is asked to respond to questions such as "In how many ways can you move across this balance beam?" or "How can you cross this room using any three parts of your body?"

Exploration in the open setting also includes an intense sensory involvement with the surroundings. Children learn through different modalities. Students who are most receptive to stimuli processed visually need to use pictures, filmstrips, charts, and posters. Other learners who respond better to auditory presentations ought to spend a large share of their time at a listening center with records and tape cassettes. Still other students who need kinesthetic and tactile activity to consolidate their learning profit best from the use of their hands, arms, and entire bodies in both large-muscle and small-muscle activities. They need to be allowed to change freely their positions, locations, and tasks. They should be encouraged to use heads, hands, feet, and other body parts while tracing difficult spelling words, while making letter forms in penmanship class, or while learning about geometric shapes in mathematics studies.

Sensory exploration also suggests that children become more acutely aware of their environment through their senses of smell, touch, and taste. Children in open schools tend to spend much time out-of-doors; they may be taking walks to examine the natural world, collecting materials to bring back to the classroom for closer inspection, simply savoring the joy of being alive on a crisp autumn afternoon, enjoying the hush of the first winter snow, or marching through puddles in the middle of spring.

Finally, exploration shows the child the validity and the importance of his own experiences. How he has reacted to his surroundings is an essential ingredient in his painting, his oral and written compositions, his response to great literature, and his appreciation of music and dance. The open teacher asks her students to recall personal experiences and to integrate them in daily assignments. In all activities the child-explorer comprehends by doing and perfects by performing, rather than by listening endlessly to the teacher talking and telling, but never allowing him to live what he is learning.

Learning How to Learn: Process, Not Product

The child in the open class discovers by fully and freely examining his environment that the processes of learning are far more important than the products of learning. Much has been written recently about the changing occupational demands on the younger generation of wage earners. The bulk of general and specialized information is increasing at a prodigious rate and technical requirements are in a constant state of flux. Facts learned today will be outdated tomorrow. Open teachers know that children need not only to know, but to know how to know. "Learning how to learn" is the phrase reflecting this new approach to education. The child cannot master the tools of learning unless the teacher believes that the method of inquiry and the motivation for exploration are far more important than the mere mastery of facts.

The open learner is relieved of much of the trivial information that customarily has been a major part of the schools' expectations. It is no longer essential for the student to memorize all the capitals of the South American countries, the principal products of Egypt, or the boundaries of Tennessee. It is more important for the geography scholar to know how to use an atlas effectively because the boundaries of countries change and the products fluctuate with the times. Similarly, a close familiarity with a dictionary and a pride in spelling improvement is more valuable than a mastery of a list of "demons." In addition to stressing the crucial reference skills that are the heart of inquiry training, the open teacher emphasizes such higher-order thinking abilities as problem solving and critical evaluating rather than memory and recall, understanding relationships instead of accumulating trivia; and developing attitudes and values in place of stressing superficial comprehension skills.

As a part of this shift toward learning and away from teaching, the child is free to inquire to the limits of his curiosity. All questions are answered openly, honestly, frankly, and comprehensibly. If there are several possible solutions to a query, the child is urged to find the explanation most meaningful to his own experiences. If there are no definite answers, the teacher readily admits her ignorance and the child is encouraged to continue his quest. Variances in information are accepted and analyzed. Facts are shown in their objectivity, and opinion is revealed in its relativity. The open teacher poses "Why?" and "How?" questions far more frequently than those with "Who?" or "Where?" or "When?" To further stimulate intellectual activity answer questions with other questions, being careful not to frustrate any child's determination to discover the truth.

Flexibility in Planning

Flexibility of materials and curriculum governs the actual classroom organization. Equipment is rearranged in response to specific student needs, and as different learning areas are set up and dismantled, clusters of chairs and tables are shifted from place to place. Students freely change their locations and positions so that several different pupils may share a single work space during the day. The content of the curriculum and the topics in a course shift as group interests direct. The furniture is diversified and partitions dividing areas are movable, allowing large areas of open space or enclosed cubicles for private thought.

Flexibility is built into the daily schedule as well. No longer does learning begin and end only with the ringing of a bell. At any moment during the day children may be working on different assignments, although there are also other times when the group focuses collective attention on a single common task. Periods of study are longer and more responsive to individual students' decisions regarding the amount of time needed for assignments and the order in which tasks are completed. The open teacher, not tied to a mandatory sequence of studies stipulated in a guide or a teacher's manual, is aware that the urgency of situations may require sudden detours in her planned program. She is alert to the promise and the potential of the teachable moment, and she knows that learning delayed may be learning denied.

Sensitivity and Affective Awareness

A marked difference between traditional and open teaching is that the open teacher is as interested in the child as a person as she is in him as a learner. This does not imply, of course, that there is not adequate time given to the many cognitive and psychomotor tasks for which the teacher has historically been responsible. However, in the open classroom the quality of being is more important than the knowledge of facts.

A large share of instructional time is spent in developing positive attitudes concerning each subject of study. For instance, in open reading instruction the child views himself as a competent reader with worthwhile capabilities, experiences, and choices. His interests are respected as he personally selects books to use, and as his original stories are included in the classroom collection of reading materials. The development of an attitude toward reading that will insure his lifelong involvement with books is a task with a higher priority than the mastery of technical reading skills. The open teacher knows that the child who does not have good feelings about himself and about reading may never read a book for pleasure. Similarly, the child who does not enjoy art, music, movement exploration, or poetry for their own sake in school is not likely to experiment with creative expression after leaving school. The child who learns facts about the world but develops no concern for the values of other people has largely wasted his social studies time. And the child who is technically proficient at mathematics and science operations but shows no curiosity about the natural world has effectively negated the efforts of his teachers. The child who sets push-up records in gym class but who as an adult does not respect his own body has really not learned much about physical education. What these examples indicate is that the child who learns only to know without learning to value has not learned at all.

In addition to sensitizing students in subject areas, the open teacher is concerned continually with interpersonal relationships, including her interactions with her students and their responses to each other. The open teacher participates in the feelings of her children so that their fears and anxieties become her own, and she shares their joys and laughter. She reacts to her pupils with the same measure of courtesy and respect that she desires from them because she realizes that her example of caring for others is a powerful model to the members of her class. She demonstrates a desire to trust by expecting her children to assume personal responsibility for their own learning and their own behavior. She minimizes mistakes and forgives slights. She is a careful listener to conversations of children. She capitalizes on the affective learning potential in sudden situations—the stolen pencil, the skinned knee, the fight on the playground, the death in the family, or the loss of a pet.

Success and Satisfaction

In the open classroom the emphasis is always on the positive. The teacher stresses what each child *can* accomplish rather than what he *cannot* do. The traditional teacher, however, often engrossed in finding errors and in correcting mistakes, sets arbitrary standards for passing grades, thereby confirming the notion in the minds of many pupils that they are "failures" if they don't pass. And since a child's self-image strongly influences his desire to learn, this child-failure soon learns to perform only routinely, marking time to the end of school, doing just enough to get by. Lacking any real zest for learning, he drops out of school intellectually long before he drops out of school legally.

Sensitivity to the need for success is demonstrated by the open teacher in many ways. When she evaluates pupil work, instead of red-penciling papers she suggests places where mistakes have occurred and challenges the students to find and correct their errors themselves. She also permits children to work in pairs or in clusters to check each others' progress. She gives many more comments that recognize achievements than those that point out inadequacies. Remarks such as "You are really making a fine effort," "You have a good imagination," or "Can you show me how this paper could be neater?" are much more supportive than statements like "This paper is a mess," or "Can't you remember anything about grammar?" When marking test items, the open attitude is shown by counting correct answers rather than incorrect ones. The open teacher modifies behavior by noticing and commending acceptable conduct rather than by carping at the problem child.

The open teacher also helps children experience success by exploring each student's background to discover individual gifts that can be integrated into the instructional program. A child with a special expertise sees he has something to share with his peers, and as an "assistant teacher" he assumes a collegial relationship with his instructor. This search for special abilities is intense and the rewards are varied. Special recognition may consist of something as ordinary as a certificate for the child to cherish, a consultant's shingle to place on his desk, or a personal chart on which he itemizes "Things I Can Do." When a child masters skills beyond those which he has brought to school, he participates in the reward system along with every other child in the room, regardless of the level of achievement or ability.

Pupils attain success also through the setting of personal goals. Students are encouraged to set their sights on objectives which are easily reached, and then to modify these goals as the students gain confidence. These individual targets can be long term and general, or they can be day-by-day and explicit. As applied to spelling, for example, the child is challenged to state the number of words he would like to try to spell correctly each week; he then selects his own list, choosing items from his compositions, from related subjects, and from standard spelling lists.

As he masters these words, he maintains a chart showing his progress. He checks off the words learned and recycles those which he needs to practice further. He does not participate in highly competitive lessons and spelling bees because no two students are responsible for the same word stock.

As the child works toward his personal goals, the teacher may suggest raising the levels of competency, rather than stress perfection as the only standard of achievement. On an arithmetic test, for instance, she may ask the learner who normally solves only ten problems to choose any fifteen of the twenty-five problems to solve, and assure him that he can work the problems again if he fails to perform at the level suggested.

The concern for success and personal achievement does not mean, of course, that the child does not develop a realistic sense of what he can and cannot do. Each child should know his limitations and should be able to live with them. If he sees himself as a fairly competent person and realizes that his out-of-school accomplishments may be more important to the teacher than his achievements in the classroom, he will be better able to live with his inadequacies. In the open setting the pupil sees that failure is only the inability to live up to the expectations of someone else, and he also understands that errors are nothing more than opportunities for further learning. The open teacher models an appropriate attitude about fallibility as she treats her own mistakes with the touch of lightness they generally deserve. This healthy approach, coupled with the opportunity for experimentation, gives the less-than-brilliant child confidence to persevere despite his mistakes and misunderstandings.

Finally, the open classroom is characterized by a pervasive sense of happiness born of satisfaction. Joy is generated by pleasant surroundings. With a little imagination anyone can change even the most ordinary classroom into an attractive place to learn. The use of color and textures and informal furnishings can help children be proud of their classroom. Joy is also the product of a spirit of play. Sometimes simply the changing of nomenclature can develop a different point of view; there is no reason why a worksheet cannot be called a "puzzle page," or why a review exercise might not be referred to as a "fun sheet." Too, there are dozens of high-interest children's games—from "Anagrams" to "Zip"—that can easily be adapted to learning experiences. Joy is also present where there is humor and smiling and laughter. The open teacher, recognizing the release provided by jokes and riddles, makes a place for them in her daily routine and reserves an important display area for cartoons, clever sayings, and nonsense verse. She laughs at herself, she appreciates a wry twist of words, and she uses a smile, a nod, and a pat on the back to show each of her students that she cares.

chapter two
Some Optional Conditions in Open Settings

In counterpoint to the preceding eight principles that are essential in open class-rooms, there are several optional conditions that figure prominently in discussions of this important topic. These include open space, multi-age grouping, team teaching, ungradedness, and the integrated day. Each of these five elements involves an organizational scheme. It is important not to mistake them for the underlying principles of openness because the teacher who looks for her success in a set of external circumstances may become disillusioned when the physical arrangements are changed. The real essence of openness continues to lie in the basic attitudes of the teacher, in her sensitivity to children as people, and in her receptivity to change. If, as a natural expression of the teacher's well-considered philosophy and her dedication, certain optional conditions can be worked out, they indeed have much to offer children.

Open Space and Open Learning

The term "open space" refers to the practice of removing the interior walls from an instructional area and rearranging furniture inside the classroom to provide flexibility and variety in the instructional setting. Because "open space" has sometimes mistakenly been used as a synonym for "open education," situations may arise in which a principal, while showing visitors around a new school, points with pride to a large open area and announces "We have an open school," thereby suggesting that the use of space itself ensures open learning. The fact is, however, that openness demands much more than the judicious use of space; openness requires a professional predisposition toward learning and children that has very little to do with classroom arrangements. It is even possible for a teacher who understands the principles of openness to develop good instruction in a closet, if she has nowhere else in which to teach. Openness does not depend on open space, although the appropriate use of space is important in providing alternative learning experiences in the open situation.

Another important point to remember is that some teachers feel insecure when walls disappear. In an open space where there is a considerable flow of students, distracting noise, and clutter and confusion, it is not surprising to discover some teachers sequestering themselves in the private corners of a large area and erecting psychological barriers that are just as real and just as confining as partitions made of brick and wood. This is all the more lamentable when the permanent removal of walls sacrifices flexibility and makes it impossible to close the open arena when it becomes necessary to control light, traffic, and noise. The problem of too much open space suggests that when new buildings are built or when old ones are remodeled, there is a need for "open-able" space, rather than "open" space.

A sad irony in American education is that the teachers who must use instructional space are rarely involved in planning it. School buildings are largely the products of school boards, architects, and administrators who, responding to fads in education, sometimes fail to provide a plant that is sufficiently flexible to serve different and changing needs. In this regard it is interesting to note that in England today some of the very best open educating is occurring in monstrous outmoded Victorian piles of school buildings, many of which serve as a sharp contrast to the shiny, modern, carpeted warehouse-like schools being built in the United States.

Opening space in the traditional building or creating a brand new open school produces open learning only if the professionals involved in the decision making insure that the form of their classrooms follows the functions that are to be conducted inside the structure. An open space which is well planned and well supervised offers a measure of mobility that open learning certainly can use. Open space serves the child's frequent need to choose where he wants to be, and it accommodates the variety of learning centers and media that must be readily accessible to the student. In the traditional classroom the child is much more likely to be restricted to the single self-contained classroom and to a common set of materials and media, but the open area permits the learner to sample a wider selection of locations and learning experiences. Furthermore, the open area allows the development of smaller spots inside the larger one, thereby giving greater privacy to individual pupils. The open classroom can include personal carrels, acoustically treated to permit quiet reading or thinking; sight barriers to reduce distractions for small group instruction; varied lighting to direct children's attention to different learning centers; irregular nooks and crannies offering security for independent inquiry; movable partitions that modify the flow of traffic; varied ceiling and wall surfaces to add visual interest and to control noise; multiple levels of work surfaces so each child can work comfortably on the floor, at a table or a desk, or on a platform raised off the floor.

Multi-Age Grouping: Potential for Progress

Multilevel grouping is a means of incorporating in one instructional setting a group of children whose ages encompass a two- or a three-year span. For instance, children of age five, six, and seven may be assigned to one classroom under a single teacher, or children of eight, nine, and ten may be placed in the care of several professionals working as a team. The cluster approach is also sometimes referred to as "family-style" grouping because in some situations a roomful of students actually does include two or more learners from the same home. The term "family grouping" is also used to suggest a degree of interdependence and mutual help between younger and older children which is reminiscent of the relationship that ideally exists in the family unit.

Multi-age grouping to achieve a wide range of ages is not essential for open education, however, because any teacher in any self-contained traditional classroom finds at any single grade level a cluster of children with differing ages. For example, every kindergarten teacher at the beginning of the school year discovers she has enrolled several children who are not yet five years of age; she also customarily has in attendance a number of students who have just turned five, along with others who are five and a half; there are also likely to be several other pupils who are almost six years of age at the start of her fall term. This full-year difference between the youngest and the oldest child is the case in almost all American schools, and although there is no close correlation between a child's age and his general school achievement, this chronological spread can help to account for some of the variability found in all classrooms. The age range can help the open teacher to develop her own family approach even if she is teaching in a self-contained room because the concept of older helping younger is valid wherever there is an appreciable gap separating firstborn and last-born children. However, it is more important to remember that the intellectual and social differences among children go far beyond those accounted for by the calendar: some of these same kindergarten children may have mental and group skills characteristic of the four-year-old, and others may act more like six- and seven-year-olds.

In view of the obvious variations in human nature already present in the self-contained classroom, many open teachers question the usefulness of deliberately increasing the spread by introducing into the same setting an even wider age span than one would ordinarily find. However, although openness does not depend on multi-age grouping, there are many situations in which it can work well. One important consideration in favor of the family-style approach is that it might allow a teacher to work with one group of children for more than one year, although even the self-contained teacher might also request that same privilege. The advantages of a long-term relationship between a teacher and her pupils are apparent: the teacher gets to know more deeply each child; there is greater continuity in planning, with less overlapping and repetition; and there is less orientation required as the students come to class every autumn. In some instances multi-age grouping is arranged to induct a small set of young children each fall, making it possible that in any one room only one-third of the students will be new at the start of a school year. In some open classrooms it may be possible for members from the same home to be enrolled in the same classroom, thereby making the group a family in the literal as well as the figurative sense. When such combinations of siblings are permitted, it is essential to develop a personalized instructional program that minimizes the competitive urges that so often exist among brothers and sisters. If multi-age grouping allows a child to remain with a certain teacher for more than one year, or if the class includes siblings, the teacher ought to consult with the parents and the children involved as a precautionary measure; and either the teacher, the parent, or the child should be allowed to elect some other class placement.

Multi-age grouping sometimes offers greater flexibility in developing various relationships among children than is found in traditional classes. Because abilities vary much more widely in a multi-age class than they do in a single-age group, the open teacher is able to introduce a greater variety of learning experiences by encouraging work on many levels of ability. She is also better able to have older children help explain difficult concepts to younger learners. Further, the multi-age involvements in classrooms more nearly approximate the natural arrangements of children in out-of-school situations. Children who find themselves in mixed-age clusters on the playgrounds or in backyards tend to discover appropriate roles and relationships, and each person functions at the intellectual, physical, and social level at which he is most comfortable.

Possibilities in Team Teaching

Teaming is the assignment of two or more teachers to cooperative situations in which they share the responsibility for planning and implementing the instructional program. Teaming is a very timely topic in educational circles, and many schools are mandating this kind of joint classroom task.

So much has been written lately about team teaching that many persons think of teaming as an integral part of open education. Although it must be admitted that teaming is often useful in open teaching, teaming should not be considered imperative in the open setting. It is important to recall that team teaching can work to the disadvantage of adults and children alike. Some teachers, for instance, are quite capable of working alone but find it impossible to work cooperatively with other adults because they have been trained to approach their job with a proprietary air, grade-level materials, grade-level concepts, a liking for enclosed classroom space, and the feeling that whatever happens in the rest of the school is of no immediate concern. When the day begins, these teachers like to close the door and to hang on it a "Do Not Disturb" sign for the rest of the day. Many very capable teachers lack the self-confidence to work with other professionals in a close relationship, or else they have personality quirks that make teaming impossible.

Another negative consideration is that many children find it hard to adjust to a teamed approach which requires that they shift their loyalties from teacher to teacher and change their behaviors and attitudes to accommodate the expectations that necessarily vary from one adult to another. Some children, especially those who come from homes where they do not feel secure, need to relate to one dominant figure; team teaching tends to deny these children that strong relationship.

Still another problem occurs when the administration imposes teaming on the entire faculty instead of developing it through the initiative of individual instructors who desire to work together. Mandatory teaming forces teachers to work in a situation that itself contradicts individual choice, one of the key concepts of the open approach. When a no-choice arrangement is imposed on teachers, the shared relationship often demonstrates only the most superficial levels of cooperation, expressed by teachers' comments such as "I'll teach reading and you teach mathematics." Such an approach fragments the curriculum, stresses convenience rather than mutuality of concerns, and focuses on subjects rather than on children. There is always the latent possibility that such teaming might turn teachers into subject matter specialists rather than develop them into experts on learning.

A fourth difficulty with team teaching is that it sometimes involves an elaborate administrative scheme of differentiated staffing in which complex organizational charts are outlined and team leader responsibilities and roles are identified. Labels spring up in response to job descriptions and a whole army of quasi professionals get involved: cadet teachers, lead teachers, master teachers, provisional teachers, senior teachers, special teachers, teacher interns, teacher assistants, and team leaders. Unhappily, when such organizational plans rigidify teaching, when job titles and descriptions generate additional layers of bureaucratic overburden, when there is no room in a school for a highly individualistic teacher who would rather work by herself, team teaching loses its appeal.

Team teaching best serves open education when it is voluntarily entered into by people who find themselves to be compatible in their approaches to teaching and in their goals for children, if there is consensus in the need for teaming, if children are consulted regarding their own involvement in a teamed classroom, and if the team approach is renewable periodically by each person participating in it. The advantages teaming offers are obvious when one considers what two or more professionals can offer in a harmonious effort. First, the use of a team permits a more diversified approach to instruction. "Two heads are better than one," says the proverb; this is aptly illustrated as the team compares and pools their experiences, their training, their resources, and their techniques. Each teacher has her own background and her own strengths which can be realized in her classroom performance, so that with a team of teachers the pupils should emerge with a greater complement of studies than they would find in a single teacher class. A teaching team can use special interests to help provide a balanced program that otherwise eludes the solo teacher who was never particularly good at mathematics, who sees herself as unartistic, or who stresses literature at the expense of the other subjects for which she is responsible. Teaming also minimizes the duplication of planning and expenditures for materials.

Team teaching allows ample flexibility in scheduling. Doubling up on supervision means that some children can be learning outdoors while others remain inside or that some children can be involved in one type of learning activity while other students are busy at a completely different set of tasks in another classroom. Children have many options as they move from teacher to teacher, soliciting different opinions, defining their relationships, responding to the expertise of each teacher, and adopting for their own lives the examples of cooperation and consideration they see demonstrated by the professionals present. Under teamed instruction children also have a more nearly complete selection of social opportunities available. Where two or three times the normal number of children cluster together, any child multiplies the likelihood of his finding compatible friends, effective workmates, and like-minded acquaintances whose interests and ambitions coincide with his own.

Ungradedness: Pro and Con

Ungradedness is the practice of eliminating grade-level designations from the schools and substituting a series of minilevels of instruction through which the children must progress. The ungraded arrangement is found most commonly in primary schools, and most often the reading program is the key to its implementation. Ungradedness at the primary level sometimes includes nine or more levels of general competency through which each child passes in his first three years of all-day schooling. If a child has trouble learning, he may spend a fourth year in the program before continuing on to the middle grades. Proponents of ungradedness argue that the grade levels found in the traditional school are really there for nothing more than administrative convenience and that the practice of retaining children in grades does not serve the needs of the slow learner. Similarly, the more able student should be allowed to move more rapidly through a sequence of instructional tasks, rather than be forced to learn at the rate of slower pupils in the room.

It is not surprising that ungradedness, with its emphasis on continuous progress, has become closely identified with open education. To be sure, openness does incorporate some of the concepts associated with ungradedness. However, it is not appropriate to assume that classes must be organized in ungraded levels before open learning can occur. On the contrary, even in a school that is organized in traditional grade levels, an effective teacher can develop open learning.

Further, there are certain problems connected with ungradedness that may confuse even the most knowledgeable and well-intended open teacher. One of these difficulties is that the minilevels designed to provide continuous progress may themselves become just as structured and just as inflexible as the grade levels they are intended to replace. It may become almost impossible for a slow child to progress through the various levels of increasing difficulty, and he may need to be promoted on the basis of social considerations rather than his intellectual attainment. When the minilevels represent a set of minimum essentials that all pupils must master equally and alike, the ungraded approach tends to overlook the variability of human nature. One more point of confusion is that not all learning occurs in neat developmental sequences, moving from simple to complex concepts and skills. Rather, children in natural environments tend to grow in spurts, pausing on plateaus between these surges. They like to try difficult tasks, and they intersperse challenging activities with easier ones, rendering placement on appropriate levels difficult and in opposition to openness. Another drawback associated with ungradedness is that it generally depends for its success on grouped instruction. Although grouping is not inconsistent with openness, grouping should be done only in proper balance with individualized learning; ungradedness often creates an imbalance in favor of group instruction. Also, when grouping for ungraded experiences shifts children to appropriate ability groups, it may contribute to the embarrassment of older pupils who are required to work with younger children at a common level, especially if the rooms themselves and the materials they contain are labeled specifically for less able students.

Although traditional grade-level designations are not obstacles to open education, ungradedness can be useful in helping children move more smoothly through their learning experiences. It is important to remember, however, that open learners should be able to move in several directions. Although the typical progress of students is represented as a vertical ladder, with children moving upward from rung to rung, the best ungraded approach is that for which the most appropriate analogy is a tree. The child is able to branch out into many related areas, perpendicular to or generally paralleling the growth expected of others who are his age. This "tree of knowledge" comparison also allows for three other kinds of development: an expansion of his present understandings at a constant level of competency, regression to concepts he did not completely master, and a condition of stasis in which a learner can repeat the same learning experiences either to recapture their excitement and joy or to gain greater self-confidence.

Examining the Integrated Day

"Integrated day" refers to the removal of schedules and other artificial barriers to learning, making it possible for a child to spend all of his day in independent learning activities that tie together all related curriculum areas. Specific time slots are not needed in the integrated day, and the learner takes the initiative in making commitments for keeping constructively occupied in a wide selection of topics and materials.

In some ways the integrated approach does make considerable sense. If the principal responsibility for learning is to be entrusted to the child, the arbitrary boundaries of time and space lose their significance. And it is true that the child, in play and other informal activities, does not divide his out-of-school time into arbitrary periods, each with its appropriate label. Instead, he pursues interests to their logical conclusions, chooses activities in keeping with his capabilities, accepts challenges that he is comfortable with, makes connections between the phenomena in his own private world. When the child comes to school, however, curriculum specialists, legislative committees, and administrators have already specified that certain shares of his time must be spent in quest of stipulated concepts, information, and skills.

The open teacher, therefore, must reconcile two pressures: first, the need of the child to fulfill his personal interest and inclinations; and second, the demands of society to produce educated citizens. Because there is a need for compromise, the fully integrated day is neither possible nor necessary in a successful open classroom, even though open learning is best when it is integrated to a great degree. The open teacher should be able to correlate studies in two or more subject areas to make combined use of two or more periods of the day. In both traditional and open schools the realities of scheduling are such that certain blocks of study time must be arbitrarily designated. Special teachers for physical education, music instruction, art, speech therapy, and remedial assistance all need to work with children at pre-determined periods during the week. Other management considerations include children's assigned times on playgrounds, in cafeterias, and other commitments. Though it is true that it is not always possible to integrate studies period by period or subject by subject, the open teacher allows her students to move freely from topic to topic, from medium to medium, and from place to place. When reviewing her unencumbered time, she arranges for large chunks of uninterrupted study suitable for intensive and extensive explorations. Within this large block of time she suggests modules and mini-units that encourage independent investigation.

chapter three
Facts versus Fallacies in Informal Learning

In view of the widespread interest in open education, it is not surprising to discover a number of comments made about openness that are not founded on fact. As with any new school practice or philosophy, opposition to openness has arisen. Even in England, the birthplace of the open approach, controversy and rejection have occurred. There is much concern in both England and America that somehow open education is leading children away from the "basics" and that the new ways of teaching are tainted with permissiveness, progressivism, and radical thought. There is genuine fear that open techniques are not appropriate for most children attending schools in America. Because there is much misunderstanding, it is important that several false arguments be put to rest.

Can Young Children Be Open Learners?

Fallacy: Since open education requires a high degree of pupil direction and responsibility, it is not appropriate for young children.

Facts: Openness is especially useful for young children. For one thing, because a person is most impressionable at this age, attitudes and habits that are learned in the preschool and the early school years are those that last the longest and affect the child most profoundly. To delay the advantages of open education until the child is older is to suggest that his participation in democratic training is something that cannot occur until he is well past his most receptive years. In reality, the child at the very earliest opportunity should be involved in helping make his own decisions and in taking responsibility for his own achievements. Even a toddler wants to help himself, and this desire for independence is just as characteristic of nursery, kindergarten, and primary children as it is of much older students. When a child's participation in his own educational decision making is delayed, he learns that his wants and his opinions are not useful. He also learns not to display any initiative, but to wait instead for his teacher to direct him. Openness also stresses that every individual is unique. Attitudes about self-respect and respect for others need to be shaped early if a child is to become a useful citizen. Further, as his accomplishments are noted and as his initiative is encouraged, the young child begins to see himself as a wholesome and worthwhile individual. The young child generally offers a refreshing eagerness to learn, a natural motivation to attend school, and candor and simplicity that are sometimes not found in older students. He is more responsive to the excitement of schooling, for he has not, as yet, experienced the challenge of outside activities that capture the attention of older pupils. The young child has not been conditioned against exploring his world, he is less afraid to try something new, and he is not as likely to view himself as a failure. Because open education capitalizes on children's natural tendencies, to delay the fulfillment of the child by denying him close involvement with openness is only to make the task of teaching the older child that much more difficult.

There is, of course, much in open education that recommends it to older children as well. The most obvious advantage accruing to older pupils is that their study skills and reading abilities enable them to handle independent learning more readily than can their junior counterparts. Older students follow written directions more easily, operate more sophisticated equipment, record more accurately the results of their learning, and can work outside the school building without direct adult supervision. However, even the nursery school child can be entrusted with the job of choosing an activity or a set of materials for his own investigation; the kindergarten child can operate simple machines when given adequate directions; and the primary child can evaluate his own progress. No child is too young to play an important role in directing his own education.

Openness and Atypical Children

Fallacy: Open education works only with children who are either average in their abilities or above average.

Facts: Open techniques can work for all children, including those from disadvantaged homes, those with learning problems, and those with special talents who do not respond well to conventional instruction.

Disadvantaged children benefit from openness because the open teacher provides experiences that compensate for the support and encouragement that many underprivileged students fail to get at home. One important contribution of the open classroom to any child is a healthier self-concept. The disadvantaged child often suffers at the hands of the traditional teacher whose culture and whose values vary so markedly from those of the students in her care. In this classic confrontation the disadvantaged child knows that he is competent in his own neighborhood and knows his role in his family, but the materials he is given in the traditional classroom, and the skills he is expected to master, often do not relate to his own experience. He repeatedly fails to satisfy the teacher's expectations; he loses confidence in himself; he sees little relationship between the classroom and the real world as he understands it; consequently, he resorts to unruly behavior to reassure himself or to gain public notice. His goals are not well defined, so he sees no special merit in persevering with his formal learning, especially when he finds himself well behind his peers and unable to meet grade-level standards.

Teachers succeed with disadvantaged children when they apply open techniques. Open teachers stress individual student's accomplishments rather than emphasize what slow learners cannot do. They solicit pupils' opinions and choices, thus developing their sense of self-worth. In cooperative planning with their students open teachers draw the attention of the disadvantaged children to realistic and long-term goals, as well as to immediate objectives. The open teacher also offers this child a measure of personal attention he does not receive at home, where many members of the same family may continually vie for recognition. Further, the informal arrangements of open settings afford the child a measure of privacy he may not enjoy anywhere else.

The transformation of the disadvantaged child from a frustrated individual to a self-directed and satisfied learner does not happen overnight. This type of student is often mistrustful of teachers and other authority figures. He may find the informal routine and the lack of general structure unfamiliar and may require a more gradual introduction to decision making. He may mistake the teacher's indirect methods as a sign of weakness, just as he may mistakenly assume that the lack of physical control reflects indifference on the part of the adult in charge. Given adequate time, however, an open classroom helps show the child that he is truly somebody, that his experiences are worth writing and talking about, that he is respected and listened to, and that he can make a substantial contribution to the class and to the community at large.

Remedial students in traditional schools are generally assigned the services of a specialist for a part of the school day. Unhappily, much remediation occurs in a separate classroom set apart from the regular room. The remedial student soon mistakenly perceives that those students who are required to get help are "dumb." Too, the methods and materials of remediation may vary radically from those used by the regular teacher, and the means of evaluating progress may differ markedly. A related problem arises when remedial teachers stress grade-level achievement, reflecting an earnest effort on their part to get the slower students to work up to a predetermined competency.

The open classroom can be especially helpful to remedial pupils. One reason is that the open teacher emphasizes a diagnostic approach which assigns materials and activities to children on the basis of what they reveal of themselves. It is easy to accommodate the needs of these special children within the regular classroom because during much of the day all students are working on different assignments. Thus the remedial child is not singled out as being dramatically different from his peers just because he uses a certain type of learning medium or consults with a resource teacher. In open schools remedial specialists spend much of their instructional days in many different locales. Their most urgent task is to find materials that suit the needs of each pupil, rather than to subject all children to the same materials.

Several types of problem learners other than remedial students are now a part of the special education programs in schools throughout the nation. Classroom teachers today are well aware of the needs of children with a variety of learning disabilities, and they are adapting to these needs. No longer are special children labeled, compartmentalized, and isolated from normal children. No longer are they pitied, avoided, or ridiculed. Because the open teacher encourages children to accept all persons regardless of their abilities or their appearances, the integration of special children in regular classrooms is occurring in open schools with very little notice by the normal students. The team approach is also enhanced as the special teacher is being trained to serve as another resource person and the classroom teacher is learning how to reinforce the techniques used by the specialist.

One question teachers have always asked is "What can I do with the *bright child?*" Locked into the traditional approach, the gifted child often becomes a casualty. Endless and meaningless assignments give him the notion that it is not to his advantage to work as well as he can. His original ideas are not popular with the conventional teacher. He quickly becomes bored and invents his own mischief as an outlet for his creativity or to gain attention, challenging his teacher and threatening her sense of security. In short, the gifted child at best responds in an acquiescent way to his teacher's demands, and at worst becomes a behavior problem and wastes a tremendous potential.

The open classroom is ideally suited to gifted children. The open teacher's assessment of his abilities and interests provides those activities that pique his curiosity and stimulate his thinking. He is encouraged to work independently, exploring topics that may lead him far afield and committing himself to projects in keeping with his abilities. If there are subjects in which he is more skillful than the teacher, his competence is utilized in the instructional program. When his imagination spawns novel ideas, they are nurtured. He is permitted the degree of privacy necessary to pursue his principal goals, but he is also taught to respect the accomplishments of his peers who are less talented than he is, and to live realistically within a heterogeneous social environment.

What About the Free-School Movement?

Fallacy: Open education is best expressed in free schools.

Facts: Many groups operating free schools do use important elements of openness. For example, free school students exercise a high degree of autonomy in making educational decisions. However, it should not be said that all free schools offer responsible open education. In truth, there is serious controversy among the free school proponents concerning this very fundamental question: how much autonomy should be permitted the child? It is argued that the child is essentially a noble creature and is thus endowed with qualities such as innocence and purity; as such, he should be allowed to do virtually anything he wants to do. He may not even be required to attend regular instruction, and he may have a greater voice in the governance of the school than do the adults who organized it. The ultimate expression of this viewpoint is "Every child must do his own thing."

Free school advocates who promote this philosophy are naive to assume that a democratic classroom guarantees a situation in which all persons are equally experienced, equally pure in their motives, and equally sound in their judgment. Actually, most children would rather play with their toys than learn their lessons, and most would prefer to stay at home rather than attend school. It is also true that random activity itself is not necessarily learning, that having fun is not to be equated with getting an education. The notion that the child needs to do only what he wishes to do belies the true purpose of open education—the development of personal responsibility to accompany the child's educational choices. The democratic ideal suggests that self-restraints and group considerations must accompany any definition of freedom. The effective open classroom enables the child to strike the best balance between his own desires, on one hand, and the needs of the group, on the other. There must also be an equilibrium between what the child can best learn on his own and what he can learn as a result of social interactions. Equally important, the teacher must remain the central figure in the classroom. She must use her best judgment in helping children to discover their talents, interests, and needs, she must assist them in using their time profitably, and she must enable them to establish reasonable boundaries for their behavior.

Open Education and Progressivism

Fallacy: Open education is nothing more than a rediscovery of progressive education.

Facts: Open education does owe a considerable debt to the movement which developed in America shortly after the beginning of this century. Unfortunately, progressive principles, though sound in theory, were widely abused in actual practice, and by the 1950s the progressive philosophy was discredited and largely abandoned. In many ways the tenets of John Dewey and other leaders of the movement were designed to serve the compelling needs of children. It would be difficult for any teacher, open or traditional, to argue against the following tenets that appeared on the masthead of *Progressive Education* as early as 1927:

> Children should be permitted a greater degree of physical movement and a wider variety of activities in the classroom.
>
> Children should be involved in making many of their own educational decisions.
>
> The expressive arts should have a greater place in the school curriculum.
>
> The natural growth of the child is important to consider in planning an instructional program.
>
> The affective needs of children are more urgent than their cognitive needs.
>
> Children should be engaged in learning that integrates knowledge and that requires cooperative involvement of many persons at one time.
>
> The best way to learn something is by doing it, rather than by reading about it or discussing it.
>
> Children are more concerned about the immediacy of the moment than the needs of the distant future.
>
> The classroom should serve as a model of a democratic society.

Sadly, the progressive ideals were never completely understood or effectively implemented by the majority of teachers in American schools. In many situations these beliefs and many like them were interpreted as a romantic way of looking at children and at learning; true sentiment for children deteriorated into sentimentality about them, and the rigor of learning lost out to a contempt for the intellectual processes. The activity-centered progressive classroom lost its point as it made no demands on students other than that they please themselves. The double disciplines of behavior and intellectual inquiry were thought to be incompatible with the need of the learner to be unencumbered by adult expectations. Progressivism eventually became equated with permissiveness, and permissiveness in rearing children came to be viewed with increasing alarm. It was no surprise, therefore, that the excesses of the movement soon outnumbered its successes and progressivism quietly faded away.

There is, of course, the same danger of oversimplifying the learning act and overestimating children's capabilities for self-government in open education as there was in Progressivism. The open teacher needs to remember that she should be "permitting" but not "permissive." She should allow children to make many personal choices, but only if those decisions will, in the long run, work for the advantage of the learner. The teacher must show children how to identify goals for themselves and to work toward those objectives—but in highly individualized ways—and she must not be afraid to intervene in the decision making of the child who lacks motivation; she should be ready to say "no" to the child who needs strong direction; and she should be constantly aware of the responsibility for instructional leadership she assumes when she signs her contract.

Has the One-Room School Been Rediscovered?

Fallacy: Open education is nothing more than a modern interpretation of what happened in the old one-room school.

Facts: There are indeed many good things to be said for the one-room school. It was the backbone of the early American education system, offering a rudimentary training that served the purposes and needs of past generations. There were certainly many outstanding teachers, and much practical learning was produced. However, to equate the potential of open education with what is hazily remembered as the best of the "good old days" is to deny the usefulness of many modern teaching techniques. The one-room school, for all its contributions to society, featured rote learning, stressed conformity of thinking, used the same materials year after year, demanded stern teacher-dominated discipline, and offered only those experiences that could be handled through textbooks, chalk, paper, and pencil. The one-room school could never be compared with the open classroom in which the teacher stresses meanings and relationships rather than memorized facts, learners capitalize on their own interests and abilities, standards of conduct are jointly developed in the light of communal needs, and students are flooded with materials and experiences that make their learning relevant to the community at large. If the old-fashioned school was really the equivalent of today's open school, where was the variety of techniques for recording and reporting pupil progress? Where was the flexible use of furniture and space? Where were self-selection, self-pacing, and the student's responsibility for self-assessment? Where did the teacher allow exploration and discovery instead of telling her students all they needed to know? Where did the pupils learn to think creatively?

It is fair to admit that much of what constitutes openness today is simply good pedagogical procedure that is timeless in its applications. To the extent that the individual needs of children have been adequately met, openness has always been present somewhere in American schools since the very first schoolmarm. Certainly many teachers have long been using with very little fanfare some of the elements of the open approach. Their success with openness has not depended as much on the time or the place as it has depended on their dedication to children and their understanding of the needs of specific learning environments.

Matters of Time and Money

Fallacy: Open education usually requires much more teacher time and much more school funding than does the traditional approach.

Facts: This fallacy is best refuted by pointing out that the *expenditure* of both time and money is not as relevant as their *distribution*. A dedicated teacher who already has a tremendous commitment to the clock could find it easy to think that openness would make even greater demands on her schedule. She must consider all the individual contacts with children, all the personalized planning, and all the development of learning materials. However, the fact of the matter is that there is much consolidation and saving of time made possible by the practice of entrusting to children the tasks of planning, selecting, and checking their own achievements. Traditional teachers are notably reluctant to relinquish their control of these instructional tasks, for they perceive their jobs to include all the planning, all the instructing, and all the evaluating. But in the open classroom the child is not required to report to the teacher for every correction or direction. No longer does the teacher constantly check the class with her critical and constabulary eye and ear; no more are there endless stacks of papers to grade and workbooks to appraise; no longer is the red pencil in constant use. Instead, open learners perform most of their own daily checkups, which are supplemented by an occasional mastery test administered and evaluated by the teacher. Some children need much close contact with the teacher while the more capable students require only infrequent conferences for casual evaluation. Because open learners are asked to help each other with their daily tasks, the long lines of students waiting for help at the teacher's desk are eliminated. In the open classroom pupils are allowed to work in mutually supportive pairs or clusters, and the more able students are encouraged to help their peers who need assistance from time to time.

Further time is saved because open learners are excused from the repetitive involvement in concepts and skills they have already mastered. A quick application of a diagnostic test or a pretest before a unit of study determines which children lack specific information offered in that unit. And the open teacher, using items on the test instrument as a guide, allows each child to choose only those learning activities that are designed to supply the necessary competencies. Having avoided useless replication of earlier efforts, the child has a much greater interest in his work and a healthier, more cooperative attitude about school than he might otherwise have. This greater measure of cooperation engenders better pupil conduct, and better behavior means fewer hours spent by the teacher in helping children understand their social responsibilities.

The cost of schooling is always a concern of administrators, who must allocate funds. It also concerns teachers, who never have enough money to spend, and it concerns parents and the community which must provide the finances for the instructional program. Although actual expenditures vary from one open classroom to another, the open approach, in principle, does not need to involve greater funding than does a comparable traditional classroom. Despite the fact that the proliferation of materials and equipment which often is found in the open school leads people to imagine a large outlay of funds, one-of-a-kind purchasing allows the teacher to invest small amounts of money in a much wider variety of items than she would be able to purchase in a traditional school. In the area of reading, for example, the usual traditional purchase plan is to order twenty-five sets of the same materials, one copy for each child in the room: twenty-five copies of the basal textbook, twenty-five copies of the accompanying workbook, and twenty-five copies of the supplementary reader. This conventional approach to spending reflects the attitude that all children should be exposed to the identical learning experiences. In the open setting, on the other hand, the theory of instruction suggests that children may need to be working from many different materials at any given time. The open teacher, while spending the same amount of money as does her more traditional colleague, can order perhaps a small set of basal readers for grouped instruction, spending the remainder of her funds for twenty different readers at several grade levels; or, she might choose to spend some money on library books, laboratory reading matter, or on visual aids to stimulate reading interest. By diversifying her purchases in this way she is able to multiply the variety of instructional materials tenfold or twentyfold without spending more money than does her more conventional counterpart.

Nor does openness depend on extensive and expensive remodeling of the physical facilities. Because open space is not essential to open education, walls do not need to be removed. The open teacher adapts any available space and furniture to her instructional needs. When she requires partitions, she recycles large cardboard cartons that the children decorate. She solicits from the parents and the community usable furniture which adds interest to informal learning centers, and she brightens the walls with children's cheerful artistic creations. Homemade learning materials and equipment are another source of financial savings. The open teacher encourages her children to make inexpensive learning aids from discarded or low-cost items. Most professional teacher magazines are full of ideas that can be converted by inventive adults and children into useful tools for learning. Children love to take charge of such projects, especially when they realize their handiwork is to be incorporated into the regular instructional program. Parents, too, are encouraged to participate in the open classroom as they contribute their time and their talents.

Danger! Model Schemes at Work!

Fallacy: Open education is accomplished most effectively when it is included as a part of a model organizational scheme.

Facts: As with all innovations in education, the open approach tempts teachers and administrators to think of openness in terms of charts, diagrams, and organizational schemes. It is most gratifying to impress the school board, members of the community, or visiting professionals with posters on which the entire open plan is laid out in elaborate detail. This inclination to graph the open approach is a natural one, for those who have worked hard to develop a new concept like to have some visible evidence of their efforts. However, it is well to resist this urge, for in the attempt to record permanently an organizational plan there is a real danger of crystallizing the ideas and the arrangements, thereby inhibiting the spontaneity and the flexibility that should be important parts of openness. Because open education is better described in terms of principles, enthusiasm, and concern for children, rather than in terms of conditions and job descriptions, it is wise to avoid defining concepts on charts hung on office walls.

An additional hazard in the model approach is that other teachers in other schools can easily get the idea that there is only one way in which openness can be expressed. When an open classroom becomes a formalized and replicated part of another school's plan, there is the likelihood that it will lose its novelty, its excitement, and its drive. Openness depends on the strength and the commitment of individual teachers, not on a plan that is passed along year after year, perpetuated only in picture form but not as a vital and viable concept in the minds of the professionals responsible for its success.

This cautionary note is not meant to imply, however, that interested teachers should never visit other schools to examine ways in which concepts are being developed in situations outside their own schools. Such firsthand examinations may help an open teacher to evaluate more effectively her own work. The uniqueness of each school, the singularity of every teacher, and the special needs of different students make it possible to implement openness in many different ways. If it is nothing else, openness is a personal statement made by a teacher dedicated to certain propositions; the casual observer should never too ardently follow someone else's example without first evaluating carefully what the consequences might be.

Claims of Chaos and Confusion

Fallacy: Open education causes considerable disruption to a well-ordered school day.

Facts: To the casual passer-by the open classroom may appear to be hectic and unplanned at times. There may be a higher level of noise than is generally found in traditional schools. Children may be moving about the area more freely. The children may be in the hallway working on projects, and it may seem there is no one in charge of the in-class activities. It is important to note, however, that the casual appearance of the open learning environment is generally the result of careful planning by the teacher who is still very much in control of the situation.

Because her planning now focuses on the needs of individuals, in the open classroom there may be moments when thirty or more different lesson plans are in operation simultaneously. If children can learn better from each other than they can learn directly from the teacher, they are working in small clusters. There is indeed structure and there are boundaries for behavior. But the difference is that the structure is individually determined for each child, and the children have participated in the setting of limits. The structure of the open classroom is a structure of enablement rather than one of requirement. The plans and the perimeters are designed to allow as much constructive activity as will allow each child to direct his own learning and will satisfy his need to relate to the requirements of the group. Controls are internalized rather than imposed by the teacher, and the boundaries for behavior and learning are always in the process of moving outward in keeping with the pupils' abilities to handle them.

Grouped Instruction or Individualization?

Fallacy: The ideal open classroom never involves children in any sort of grouped instruction.

Facts: Although individualized instruction is basic in the open setting, grouped teaching has many useful applications. The problem with grouping, however, is that traditional teachers tend to think that general academic ability is the only criterion for clustering children. In the conventional setting, for example, the teacher identifies reading abilities and organizes her entire year of instruction around her observation that some children are slow readers, others are average readers, while still others are fast readers. From their first school experiences pupils in traditional settings are so labeled and so assigned. Although ability grouping may be easier for a teacher to handle, it is not best—teachers tend to place students in such groups without much thought, and students may be stuck in an inappropriate group, having no recourse (being unable to appeal the decision). Children are rarely moved from one ability designation to another; and the decision of a first-grade teacher to place a child in a slow reading group may color his self-concept and shape his learning for the rest of his life. It is commonly known that such designations of students condition their thinking, so that students in the slow reading group or in remedial math tend to think of themselves as "dumb." And if academically advanced students are labeled as "gifted" or "bright," there is the danger that they may develop elitist notions.

To be effective in the open classroom, grouping must reflect several considerations. First, because grouping tends to stress uniformity rather than diversity, the teacher must be aware that even within a supposed homogeneous group of children there are still wide differences that are actually more important than the similarities present. Second, grouping only by ability denies slow students the stimulation and the leadership of faster students, and it deprives more capable students of the opportunity to relate to people less gifted than they are. Further, any form of grouping should be used flexibly and temporarily. Children should be allowed to move in and out of groups freely, at their own behest or at the suggestion of the teacher. No student should ever feel locked into any kind of instructional arrangement.

Although grouping is most commonly determined by intellectual ability, children can also be clustered according to their expressed interests. For example, a short-term reading group might be organized among all those persons in the room who enjoy books about horses. Such a group would likely represent a wide range of reading abilities, but there could be an active interchange of ideas and experiences focused on the topic. Some children might share pictures they have drawn, others might read aloud to their classmates, while still others might prefer to dramatize a story. Social studies interest groups could be organized around common hobbies: one group of children who are enthusiastic about stamps from South America, another set of pupils who are investigating music of the Pampas, and a third group of students who are weaving raffia baskets suggested by products of the Incas.

Another way to group children in open classrooms is by specific skills. As the teacher works with her pupils individually she finds certain instructional needs common to several members of the class. She can provide more efficient personal attention for such children by clustering them so that four children having trouble with digraphs in reading, several students needing assistance in dividing with decimals, or a set of six-year-olds requiring extra practice in the preprimer can work together. Children may also be grouped by social preference. In the open classroom the child has much freedom in selecting his study companions, and learning often goes more smoothly when compatible classmates interact. Such a self-chosen set might work on a project such as a mural or a play. A social preference group might also comprise children coming from the same neighborhood, or it might develop into a mutually supportive mini-unit within the larger class, taking responsibility for matters such as attendance, checking papers, administering quizzes, and serving as resource persons for others in the room.

Finally, there is something good to be said about grouping all of the children in a class. A new song can be taught to the entire group of twenty-five students just as easily as it can be taught to them one at a time. A new game may be much more fun when all the pupils are involved at the same moment. A new medium in the art corner might be presented to the total class in anticipation of later opportunities each student would have to explore it individually. The sense of class identification is also strengthened by large group activities. Each student should have several chances during the day to see that he is an important part of the group. He can take pride in belonging and can periodically renew his intentions to work for the good of the group as well as for his own personal ends.

chapter four
Adapting British Methods to American Schools

Origins of Openness in England

The fact that open education in America has been strongly influenced by British practices is readily apparent to any serious student of the subject. In 1967 Joseph Featherstone published in the *New Republic* a series of important articles which describe some especially effective new techniques he had just observed in England. Shortly afterwards the best-selling work by Charles Silberman, *Crisis in the Classroom,* provided added impetus to American educators interested in more effective measures than were being practiced. Describing most American schools as "grim and joyless places," Silberman enthusiastically pointed to the British methods as bright and promising examples of what ought to be done. The professional press reflected this discovery, and between 1970 and 1975 more than 500 articles appeared in educational journals. Hundreds of American educators have examined firsthand open schools overseas. Many colleges and universities in the United States have arranged with colleges in England to exchange teachers and teacher-trainees. Experts in British open education have traveled to this country to disseminate information about the subject.

Although the discovery in America of the open techniques has occurred only recently, there was a movement toward openness in England as early as the mid-1930s, when some of the more promising methods were generated by the Progressives. However, there was not significant growth in openness there until the Second World War when thousands of children were evacuated from the major cities and were transferred to distant towns and rural areas. In hundreds of instances British teachers accompanied their children into this educational exile and lived and worked with them for the duration of the war. Some classes met in barns or in abandoned buildings. Still others doubled or tripled the populations of small rural schools. Thousands of children attended classes on split shifts. When children remained in larger cities, teaching was often done in subways or in the shells of ruined buildings. Because there were the demands of the emergency and the resulting shortages of teaching supplies, the professionals had to rely on the materials and the experiences at hand: natural objects found in the immediate environment, discarded items that were restored to usefulness, pieces of homemade equipment, and excursions into the community or the countryside.

As much in desperation as in deliberation teachers struggling to accommodate the needs of their children discovered the suitability of a less structured approach than they had previously favored. New emphasis was placed on allowing children to assume increased shares in selecting and directing their own learning. New direction and new drive was given to creative activities, including dance, art, music, and language. Children of different ages, thrown together by the exigencies of war, discovered that there was merit in learning and living together in mixed-age groups. The rigidity of furniture and schedules fell victim to the newly found flexibility of time and space. The spontaneity of the situation prompted teachers to eliminate strict divisions and demarcations between subject areas and enabled children to see relationships that had not been apparent earlier. Teachers discovered the joy of sharing and of mutual planning, while children gained new respect for themselves when they found that their own contributions were an important part of the classroom routine. The circumstances of the wartime generation helped to shape the directions of openness today, for in the intervening years the philosophies developed and the techniques discovered almost by accident during those trying times have been refined and incorporated into hundreds of British schools.

As a recent effort in defining the role of British schools, a prestigious British committee published an evaluation of primary education in England. In this document, familiarly known as the Plowden Report, the committee identified some of the principal characteristics of the open approach and recommended their implementation in schools through the British Isles. Latest figures suggest that fewer than half the British primary schools may be correctly identified as open schools and that the schools for older children are even less committed to this new-old approach. It is important to realize that only a minority of British educators are deeply involved in openness, and it is also important to note that there are several considerations which make it unwise to transfer unaltered British methods into American schools without careful examination of differences between the two educational systems.

British Teaching and Administration

One important difference between American and British educators lies in the teacher-principal relationship. In England the local school administrator is referred to as "Headmaster," a term that strongly suggests that his role is one of "main teacher." Because the typical British school is much smaller than its American counterpart, and since the administrative details are more often tended to by clerical help, the "head" is more free to serve as a real educational leader. The major responsibility of the head is to plan and to implement an instructional program. Much of his time is spent in actual teaching—generally required by statute—which is a practice in contrast to the habit of the American principal, who spends only a small fraction of his time in actual classroom instruction. Each vacant position is advertised widely in professional journals, and the typical headmaster is chosen for his demonstrated teaching skills. The head is not promoted out of teaching as are his American colleagues; rather, he is expected to become even more deeply involved in teaching.

To discharge his instructional responsibilities the head may teach most or all of the day. He presides over the daily assembly, a traditional part of the British routine. He may work with special student groups after school, on either remedial or developmental projects. He stands in for teachers who are out of the building on released-time assignments. Since substitutes are not hired except for the more prolonged absences, he assumes part of a substitute teacher's chores as well. He participates directly in teacher education and often has responsibility for after-school in-service sessions. He generally knows the name of every child in school and in his participation in classrooms and assemblies makes a point to set the tone of the school and the climate for each day's activities. The typical head has very little training in administration, although he is looked upon as the director of the teaching team. The American principal, on the other hand, views his administrative responsibilities, the management of people and circumstances, with quite a different set of expectations from those associated with teaching children.

Once hired, the head is able to select a teaching staff that is in keeping with his own philosophy and his individual teaching style. He has much greater authority in matters of hiring and firing than is available to American principals. It is possible for the head to assemble as his faculty a group of teachers who share a common view of the nature of teaching and the needs of children. The process of selecting and shaping his staff may continue for years until the head has assembled a compatible group. The head is generally hired to a lifetime appointment by a Local Education Authority whose main functions are to select the educational leadership and to provide the support for the school program. The head enjoys a degree of security unknown in American school administration, for neither he nor his teachers experience the elaborate hierarchy of supervision that is typically found in this country. The head is not subject to extreme pressures from unions, school boards, parents, teachers, or other special interests in the community, but is viewed as a professional. He is given virtually unrestricted control of all matters pertaining to the curriculum, the behavior of children, and instructional techniques. It is no wonder that many Britons refer to a school using the name of the head rather than the given name of the institution.

Other differences are apparent in the way in which teachers are viewed. England has a long-standing tradition of leaving the teaching to the professionals, and the role of teacher is an honorable one. The national ministry in charge of schools, the Department of Education and Science, provides a variety of services to local schools, including financial support. However, since the teacher is respected, the DES does not exert direct control of what occurs inside the schools. Similarly, since local property taxes do not directly support the schools, the members of local neighborhoods do not assume that the building and its program in some way belong to the community—a proprietary attitude that seems to prevail in the United States. The DES also helps the British schools by appointing advisers who visit the heads to consult on matters of curriculum and organization. However, since the national ministry does not control the schools, the adviser is considered one who influences change by means of persuasion and logic rather than through implied threat. The adviser makes suggestions directly to the head, but he does not evaluate teachers. In addition to the advisers from the national ministry, there are local advisers supplied by the Local Education Authorities who work in schools by invitation only. They demonstrate appropriate techniques alongside the classroom instructors and present practical, short in-service courses after school to which parents as well as teachers are invited. In most instances advisers are recognized as supportive personnel rather than as another layer of supervision or another link in the chain of command.

British Governance and Support

The typical British school is small, and so it reflects the small neighborhood it serves. Bussing young children to schools is almost unknown in England, so the infant and junior schools are close to the students' neighborhood. There are very few organized attempts by parents to intervene in, or otherwise influence, the school programs. However, there is a casual relationship that exists between the parents and the school staff. Parents drop by occasionally for tea and a visit, but there are few full-scale efforts to bring parents to schools in massive visitations. Parent aides are occasionally hired to provide help with routine matters such as the preparation and the serving of meals. Although most British teachers view the parents of their children as nonprofessionals, there is not the adversary relationship that is too often found in American schools. In addition, parents do not demand the same outcomes of the educative process. American mothers and fathers expect schooling to produce social mobility for their offspring, for the democratic ideal suggests that any child can develop into whatever he wants to become. The American dream that any child can be elected President is a noble notion, but it is really not relevant to the British, who perceive much more rigidity of social classes.

Another important consideration is that while only about 10% of the British children ever continue on to college, an estimated 50% of American children do. There is thus less pressure on English schools to produce masses of students capable of performing well at the postsecondary levels. It is interesting to note in this regard that the greatest enthusiasm for open education in England has developed in working-class neighborhoods, rather than in middle-class or upper-class communities. The widespread class consciousness and respect for teachers produces in England children who are more likely to respect authority figures. As a result, British students do not require the same close supervision that American children are provided; in fact, in the British schools it is common for the teacher to leave the room from time to time, to confer with colleagues or to have a break for tea, without any real concern for possible misbehaviors of the youngsters in her care.

One final difference between the American and British systems is that Americans seem to be too quickly taken with fads in school business. The British open practices, developed over more than a generation, were given adequate time to germinate and grow. In this country there is an inclination to seek instant answers to school problems; as a result, teachers in the United States are too often the innocent victims of well-publicized trends in pedagogy that flourish briefly and then die away. Similarly, many Americans have the mistaken notion that schools can be operated somewhat like factories and that business methods can be imposed on them. This leads to an unjustified emphasis on formal testing programs, organizing students by ability only, and a growing concern about accountability and quality control.

Changing the Role of the American Principal

Although the appreciable differences between American and British systems make it impossible to impose the English methods on American schools without any serious assessment or adaptation, many of the elements of openness developed in British schools work well in any situation. Before such practices are adapted to our schools, however, it is essential to reassess and revise the roles of the persons who are most directly responsible for what happens to children in classrooms.

To begin with, the principal of any open school must define for himself a role that casts him as instructional leader in reality as well as in theory. He must involve himself personally in the daily classroom events, not only as an occasional visitor but also as an important resource person on the teaching team. Any competent principal has much to contribute to the actual learning experiences offered to children, and he must assume this challenge if he really wants to develop open classrooms. He must also be sufficiently sure of himself and confident in his faculty to allow his staff the same degree of decision making that children must be permitted. The principal needs to see himself as an enabler and a facilitator, not as a director. He also needs to reevaluate his attitudes concerning power and authority. He should view his relationship with faculty as a collegial one rather than as a supervisory one—the principal as a fellow teacher instead of a boss. His power must be the power to persuade, and the respect he gains must spring from his success in earning support instead of giving orders.

To be consistent with what should happen in open classrooms, the principal must implement and support honest experimentation in his school, even if it means making occasional mistakes. Teachers should not be locked into arrangements without their consultation and agreement. The principal must share with his teachers the procedural, budgetary, and instructional decisions. The curriculum, the building requirements, and matters of discipline must also become a joint venture in which the opinions and experiences of principals and teachers alike are respected. By allowing a variety of teaching styles, the principal should make clear that his staff members need not conform to his ideas of the best techniques, and he must demonstrate that different methods may be equally productive and may coexist in the same building.

The principal in the open school also ought to delegate much of the responsibility for routine chores, enabling him to spend a greater share of his time in consultation and in instruction. Hiring a competent executive secretary to tend to matters of bus routes, milk money, and supply orders frees him for more substantial tasks. The principal also needs to plan an effective training program which can offer a variety of resource persons and professional materials. He should be well read in the area of openness and should have a realistic appreciation of what the open approach can accomplish.

Finally, the role of the principal must also include the job of informing his public. At the very first stages of planning he must make parents aware of the proposed changes and the sound reasons for these changes. American parents take a keen interest in their schools, so it is essential that they understand how open classrooms can more effectively serve the needs of their children. There is much misinformation concerning openness, and it is important not to leave communication to chance. If the members of the community are actively involved in planning programs, visiting schools, evaluating the progress of their children, and serving as volunteer resource persons, they are much more likely to understand how openness works and much less apt to criticize rashly teachers' inadequacies.

A New Look at the American Classroom Teacher

For open education to succeed the classroom teacher as well as the school principal must make a major redefinition of her role. In the traditional sense the teacher too often sees herself as the local constable. She creates rules that govern behavior and sets absolute standards for achievement, she alone deciding whether a child passes or fails. She judges as appropriate or inappropriate each act of conduct, and she controls children's movement in the classroom and elsewhere in the school. She schedules the time of her pupils, deciding when children may use the bathroom and when they may not. Her evaluation of her students' efforts stresses the correction of mistakes. Her information is adequate for all student needs, and her authority is not to be questioned.

A close look at the teacher role that is appropriate in the open classroom suggests a number of new possibilities. One change is that the open teacher sees herself as a person who helps her pupils to find out, who asks timely questions to spur their inquiry, and who proposes many possible solutions to their problems. She is aware of many sources of information and allows her students to try without fear of failure or censure different approaches to learning. She is sufficiently flexible to change directions when circumstances recommend a shift. She reveals herself as both a fellow human and a colearner. She is an able negotiator as she helps students make their plans and record their accomplishments. The open teacher suggests alternatives, encourages exploration, diagnoses weaknesses, and discovers talents. Her gratification is in direct proportion to the extent to which each child relinquishes dependence on her daily instructions and assumes responsibility for his own learning.

Updating Teacher Training Institutions

The national interest in open education places a special responsibility on the colleges and universities where teachers are trained. An unhappy fact is that attitudes about teaching being conditioned as early as the first grades of elementary school and most children being exposed to traditional teachers, many pupils at the advanced levels enter teaching with the most restrictive notions of what they should become in this important career. After spending approximately 10,000 hours of life in situations in which they must raise hands to make a comment or ask a question, in which they are required to complete countless assignments to the specification of someone else, and in which they are tested, graded, and classified according to someone else's standards, it is no wonder that the young trainees define their professional roles in terms of the identical techniques and attitudes that they themselves observed throughout their own school experiences.

To further compound the problem, when the trainees enroll in education courses at the college level, these same courses are all too often poor examples of enlightened teaching. Professors stuff their students with facts that need to be reproduced on an examination booklet; lecturers expound tiresomely to their students; instructors do not care to know their pupils by name; courses are too superficial and too brief; and information is derived mainly from one or two textbooks. In addition, the typical teacher training program provides the trainees very little choice in selecting courses and activities that relate to their personal interests and concerns. A few colleges of education are only now experimenting with evaluation forms that identify individual competencies of their students and offer a more comprehensive comment on pupils' progress than is offered through the standard grade report. Some professors are beginning to experiment with pupil contracts and anecdotal records.

Still other shifts in techniques and roles are needed if the college training program is to produce students capable of opening classrooms across America. Each institution must provide a wealth of materials and media for trainees to examine. No longer is the teach-test-reteach approach appropriate. Textbooks must be many and varied if the teacher-in-preparation is to compare points of view. The student's interests must be cataloged and related to the ongoing instruction. Greater flexibility in scheduling and course content needs to be developed. Professors should make a genuine effort to pool their resources, their information, and their time and should be eager to work as members of a teaching team rather than as a group of individuals specializing in very narrow fields of inquiry. Opportunities for self-selected learning ought to be offered, for college students as well as kindergarteners need to learn how to set their own goals.

Changes must also occur in the ways in which in-service help is offered. Colleges should more actively assist school districts to identify and develop classrooms where openness can be practiced. Unless trainees have a chance to observe firsthand both the possibilities and the problems associated with openness, they may never be able to assess adequately its potential. Each district could have a demonstration open classroom to serve as an observation post. Outstanding teachers with a professional commitment to the open approach could staff these stations and have regular consultation from college professors who might also demonstrate especially effective techniques and suggest ways to manufacture on the spot new materials for the children enrolled. Such a consultant should be a superlative teacher capable of showing in his own college-level instruction an outstanding example of the open way.

Enlisting Community Support

Parental involvement in school planning is legitimate and essential because parents have both an emotional stake in the success of their children and a financial investment in the school plant. Most parents have had many experiences that they can contribute to help children better understand the world. They can donate materials to be transformed into learning aids and can spend their time interacting with children. Parents have many skills which they can demonstrate on a one-time-only basis. They also have those extra pairs of hands that help to manage otherwise difficult situations. Parents as partners in learning can be listeners when children practice their skills at home. Extend creative experiences introduced at school—they can reinforce in real-life situations the discoveries of their children.

One other consideration concerning parental roles has to do with parents' right to choose. In the traditional sense teaching is very much a monopolistic activity. Parents who move into a given community have no real choice concerning the school their child will attend. And once the school is determined, they have no way to select the teacher or teachers who will instruct their offspring. In effect teachers have no competition; there is no practical way to make known publicly their strengths and their weaknesses, and there is no method of dismissing an on-tenure teacher short of taking the matter to court. The open teacher should be sufficiently self-possessed and confident to permit parents to participate in matters of pupil assignment. Teachers should be much more willing to earn the respect of their clientele and should present options if parents are not convinced of the effectiveness of certain classroom procedures. This open offer would demonstrate on a very personal basis the freedom and the flexibility that are essential in open education, and it would obligate the open teacher not only to make openness work but also to communicate effectively with the parents of the students she serves.

part two
Making the Open Classroom Work

chapter five
Getting Started: Gradualism, the Key to Success

Appraising Professional Attitudes

There are so many instructional possibilities inherent in the open approach that the teacher who is not familiar with the best way to proceed may be overwhelmed with the enormity of the challenge. Mistakenly assuming that openness must be an "all or nothing" involvement, she may lose both her courage and her interest. To forestall such a misunderstanding, it is important to consider several important points. First, the teacher whose philosophy of teaching and learning is already consistent with the tenets of open education may discover that her classroom practices reflect many of the open techniques. Throughout the history of pedagogy there have always been teachers who have responded well to individual interests and needs. Such teachers today may need only to consolidate and refine their procedures and to add new methods as they gain further confidence. A second point to remember is that any significant shift from a conventional style to an open approach must be accomplished in a deliberate and an orderly way. Not even the most idealistic and most efficient teacher could ever hope to master all the possibilities that openness presents. The main ingredients in the transformation of the teacher are selectivity in choosing the elements to incorporate into her program, flexibility in her approach to the change, a continuous evaluation of her efforts, and the realization that mistakes inevitably will be made.

Perhaps the most important consideration for the teacher who is interested in becoming more open in her classroom work is for her to assess carefully her attitudes about teaching and learning, to see if they are consistent with the main assumptions about the educative process. A survey of several hundred sources on open education reveals a cluster of suppositions that recur in the professional literature. The teacher who is thinking of moving into a more informal, pupil-centered style should indicate whether or not she agrees with the thirty-four items listed in Figure 1. To the extent that her personal philosophy is consistent with the large majority of statements included in the list, her success with the open approach becomes more likely.

Figure 1   Checklist of Values

☐ The classroom should serve as a model of a democratic society, with the child assuming a major responsibility for making and implementing educational decisions.

☐ It is more important to educate a child for variety and diversity of thinking than for conformity.

☐ Helping the child to master the processes involved in learning is of greater value than his developing products of that learning.

☐ The affective and social needs of children are more significant than their acquisition of factual information.

☐ Flexibility and adaptability are important characteristics of the well-educated person.

☐ The most supportive approach to pupil errors is to treat mistakes as added opportunities for learning rather than to view them as personal failures.

☐ The child's natural tendency from the moment of birth is to explore his immediate environment.

☐ The best way to stimulate greater classroom effort is to provide situations in which children are demonstrably successful.

☐ A classroom in which little group structure exists is more likely to encourage original thinking than one in which much group organization is found.

☐ Learning through personal involvement in an experience is generally more effective than learning by listening to someone's explanation.

☐ Learning occurs more efficiently when the exploration of tangible objects precedes concept formation.

☐ Studies that are relevant to a child's past experiences and present interests are likely to be remembered longer than those that relate only to his future.

☐ Children learn at different speeds, using different modalities, and developing different styles.

☐ The motivation for learning that arises from a pupil's own experiences is more stimulating than motivation provided only by adults.

☐ Students are more likely to learn well if they are allowed to select appropriate media and materials themselves, as long as their selections are in keeping with their personal needs, interests, and abilities.

☐ Children often learn as well from each other as they learn from adults.

☐ Persons who are physically comfortable are more receptive to instruction than those who are not.

☐ Learning that comes as a result of cooperative involvement is more satisfying than that which occurs as a result of highly competitive effort.

☐ The teacher's role includes that of a fellow learner who is more advanced than her pupils in most areas of knowledge, but on the same learning continuum.

☐ The teacher should be free in the classroom to express the same human qualities she encourages in her students, and she owes them the same respect that she wants them to reciprocate.

☐ The teacher accepts willingly the total range of abilities she discovers in her students at the beginning of the year, and she labors, in part, to further widen this range.

☐ The teacher should prepare her classroom and herself for children's needs rather than expect children to get ready for her needs.

☐ The teacher is primarily a facilitator, helping learning to occur, rather than a director, making children learn.

☐ Covering thoroughly the information contained in prescribed instructional materials is less important than matching materials to individual pupils.

☐ The relationships between teacher and child should be essentially person oriented rather than role oriented.

☐ The most meaningful aspects of learning are also those that are the hardest to assess.

☐ Learning does not always occur in an orderly progression from simple concepts to more complex ones.

☐ Human knowledge and human experiences cannot be easily categorized in neat compartments.

☐ Grade level labels should be only incidental to a child's progress through school.

☐ Letter grades on a report card are among the least useful methods of evaluating pupil growth.

☐ The only true respect due a teacher is that which she earns by showing herself to be a worthy human being.

☐ The best competition for a child is that which pits him against his own past performance.

☐ Students tend to value the ideas and the rights of others as they themselves are valued.

☐ A child's self-concept strongly influences his ability to learn.

Getting Started: Gradualism, the Key to Success **47**

Selecting Pupils and Procedures

There are many kinds of potential pupil involvement in the open approach, for informality can be applied to methods, to media, to materials, to organization for instruction, or to any combination of these several elements. It is essential, however, that children's participation proceeds carefully and slowly, especially if they have not had prior experience with the options that are available to them. Reasonable precautions are mandatory because, first of all, the amount of time needed for planning and the variety of pupils' needs are such that the teacher may otherwise find herself inundated with details. Further, the teacher, in her eagerness to begin, may present to the class so many alternatives that the students may become bewildered in their decision making.

As the teacher plans the types of involvements to be used in her classroom, she should take care to identify those areas of instruction and those children most amenable to the open treatment. Children do not profit equally well from self-directed learning experiences. Each person should be carefully assessed using criteria such as his degrees of independence, general social maturity, sense of responsibility, and interest in learning. Much of this kind of information can be collected from prior records maintained by the school, or the open teacher can solicit information on simple checklists circulated among the other teachers. These efforts should reveal those children who find it difficult to accept the task of controlling their own learning, those who lose a sense of purpose without a strong teacher presence, and those who feel insecure if the grade-level designations are removed from their classrooms and their materials.

Because gradualism is indeed the key to success, each teacher should evaluate all the following possibilities and then choose the way or the ways in which she can best ease into the open style of teaching. The inexperienced teacher may attempt only one experiment with openness while the more ambitious professional may elect several. To the extent that any teacher selects even one option and uses it well, she will have succeeded in making her children's learning more effective and more interesting.

✔* *Select one independent learner.* Every classroom contains at least one child who comes to school self-motivated, eager to work, capable well beyond grade-level expectations, cooperative, anxious to please, and exhibiting a degree of responsibility that makes teaching a relatively simple task. The easiest way to begin openness is to find this one outstanding child and present to him as many of the challenges of openness as he is capable of handling without much assistance. In effect, this child can spend most of the school day and the school year on his own, keeping just enough contact with other children to maintain healthy social relationships and to enhance his own communication skills. With just a little en-

---

*The "Bright Idea" checkmark symbol (✔) is used to indicate a unique technique or activity or an especially helpful thought.

couragement such a child can progress well beyond the level of accomplishment that he might otherwise attain in a more conventional setting.

✔ *Select a high ability group.* Particularly in the primary grades children are often organized into homogeneous clusters for certain subjects. If a classroom contains several students with high potential for self-governance and achievement, they may be allowed to operate as a "class within a class," relying mainly on each other for support, direction, clarification, and evaluation, and interacting only occasionally with the teacher.

✔ *Select a single concept.* Another good method for introducing the open way is to identify one concept or one skill, to present all the informal, self-directed possibilities for involvement in that skill, and then to permit all the children in the class to participate in whatever manner they choose. For example, in science education, "Air has weight" is one discrete concept. All children in the room may be permitted to choose their specific involvements with that one idea. One child or a small group may decide to use a barometer; another may explore the siphon. Still other students may experiment with balloons and a balance, choose to view a filmstrip expanding the notion, or read a chapter from the textbook. A second example of openness in the pursuit of a single skill might occur in physical education when there may be distributed about the play area twenty different pieces of play equipment, each of which is designed to strengthen the muscles of the legs. Different children may select from options such as jumping rope, hopping over a wand, climbing a ladder, or skipping to a phonograph record.

✔ *Select one unit of instruction.* As a more ambitious application of the single-concept approach to openness, the teacher may choose a broader area of study involving perhaps several weeks of study in one subject. "Measurement" in mathematics, "Magnets" in science, and "Figures of Speech" in language arts are samples of this type of gradualism. This method gives all children a chance to explore the important components of openness in a wider range of activities and materials. As in the single-concept technique, all children are allowed to participate in self-directed learning in this one identified unit.

✔ *Select one set of materials.* Similar to the short-term single-concept approach is the involvement of all children in only one set of instructional materials. This approach is illustrated by the teacher who during reading class sets out a collection of supplementary readers and the workbooks that accompany them. All the students may use these items in highly individualized ways. Some may want to read through every story, and others may cut apart pictures from the workbooks to make practice booklets. Still other pupils may decide to tape-record some of their oral work or to share stories with younger children in other rooms. A few students may decide to complete and check all the blanks in the workbook. When the class members exhaust all the possibilities for learning represented by one set of materials, the teacher either returns to her usual formal procedures or, if she wants to continue the open processes substitutes still other sets of materials for all the students to use in a kindred manner.

✔ *Select one area of the room.* The learning center is one element frequently associated with open education. As one involvement in informal learning the teacher may identify a special corner of the room where many related materials are located. The children are told that only those items and the concepts they reinforce are available for independent work, while the other areas of the classroom remain under a more traditional type of teacher control.

✔ *Select one subject in the curriculum.* There are several studies in the curriculum that lend themselves readily to the open attitudes. Reading is one such area. Many teachers are already allowing children to individualize their reading with much self-motivated and self-directed book-and-story related learning. It is a very simple matter to open up the entire reading program for all students and to use in this one important segment of the curriculum as many informal techniques as time and interest will allow. Mathematics is also a logical subject for autonomous learning, and the expressive arts represent still another.

✔ *Select a cluster of subjects.* Some teachers may want to go beyond a single curriculum area. An obvious possibility for branching out includes those clusters of studies that lend themselves to coordinated effort. Pupil work in music, art, movement, and dance, for example, can be closely correlated. Reading and language arts are also logically connected one to the other. Mathematics and science also present interesting possibilities for correlated efforts.

✔ *Select one period of the day.* Closely associated with the single-concept approach to openness is the designation of one special time of day when all children are simultaneously engaged in self-selected activities; however, the difference between the single-period and single-concept approaches is that in the former case the children may all be working in any of the eight or ten major areas of the curriculum at the same time, rather than focusing their attention on just one small element of one subject alone, as would students involved in the single-concept approach. A part of the school day that is especially well suited to the single-period notion is the very first hour of the day. In most communities some children walk to school, some arrive in cars, while still others ride bicycles or busses. The students actually appear on the school grounds at different times. In many cases they are required to wait outside the school building under the ringing of a preliminary bell. It makes more sense to allow these children to begin their instructional activities as soon as they step onto the school grounds. In this way the teacher, who is already prepared for her duties of the day, is able to greet each pupil individually, to interact informally with him, and to plan briefly with him the learning activities for the first period. After all the students have worked at their individual tasks for that hour, the teacher calls them together for the group activities that otherwise comprise her instructional day.

✔ *Select one day.* This approach to gradual openness provides a "Free Learning Day" for the children to spend in diverse ways. The teacher announces in advance the event and suggests that the students may want to bring to school some of their own materials that might help extend their learning. Such items might be shared with other members of the class, forming a pool of one-day-only materials and activities. Similarly, all appropriate professional media available to the teacher are also on display for additional investigation by the children. Each pupil has the option of spending the day working in only one area of the curriculum or mixing and matching experiences from the entire spectrum of possibilities.

✔ *Select one philosophical consideration.* From a more theoretical point of view the teacher might select a single supposition and stress just that one element during the year. For example, she might take an assumption about teaching and learning—such as "Children often learn as well from each other as they learn from an adult"—and attempt to see in how many ways she can implement her commitment to that one point of view. Or she may choose one cardinal principle—perhaps "Open education is sensitive to the affective needs of children"—and identify specific ways in which she can reflect this statement daily. The teacher also might prefer to name one optional condition of structure and organization that is sometimes associated with open education—maybe team teaching, multi-age grouping, or open space—and work out the details of a single arrangement.

Essential Administrative Assistance

The importance of help from principals and superintendents has already been noted. Most assuredly, without their professional support for the faculty, educational leadership for the parents, and effective dissemination of information to the community, even the best-intended efforts at opening classrooms are not likely to succeed. The teacher interested in getting involved with openness might do well to assess how well she might reasonably expect backing for her efforts. Questions such as those in Figure 2 might be included in such an inquiry.

✔ When conditions are right for open teaching, the administrative staff can encourage the gradual involvement of classroom teachers in three different ways. The first method is to identify one teacher who is willing to attempt any of the open procedures, and to provide for her the physical setting and the equipment that her efforts require. ✔ A second way to ease the faculty into openness is to encourage a teaching team. If two or more teachers find themselves compatible and equally committed to the open approach, they can be permitted to operate as a minischool within the school. Such a cluster of professionals can make arrangements to share their planning, to maximize communal thinking, and to utilize the teaching strengths represented in such a group by applying them to a single grade level or extending across grade levels in formal or informal relationships. ✔ A third suggestion for encouraging open education is to set aside in a district one school in which open experimentation is to be encouraged. Such a magnet school might attract those teachers who would volunteer to teach in highly individualistic styles, each one appropriate to a personal interpretation of openness. Parents might also be permitted the option of enrolling their children in such a school. The experimental facility might also serve as the central location in the district for specialized equipment and resources that could be available to all faculty members in other schools who choose to diversify their own teaching and manufacture some of their own learning materials, whether or not they are members of a designated open education team.

Figure 2   Administrative Support and Community Attitudes Survey

☐ Are most curriculum decisions based on what is good for children rather than on the needs of adults?

☐ Is the major concern of the faculty the fulfillment of children rather than bells, schedules, grade levels, and rules?

☐ Are the members of the school board more concerned about improving instruction than saving money?

☐ Are the parents in the community generally favorable to changing teaching methods?

☐ Is there an effective communication network between the school and the parents?

☐ Is flexibility a part of the materials, courses, units of study and staff assignments used in the school?

☐ Does the faculty view the community and people in the surrounding region as appropriate resources for the children?

☐ Do the members of the administration spend more time on instructional matters than on discipline and business affairs?

☐ Is there general support for teacher's involvements in making curriculum decisions?

☐ Are parents encouraged to participate in making educational decisions and in helping to work them out in classrooms?

☐ Does the general testing program assess as many affective and social skills as cognitive achievements?

☐ Is there general respect for the individual styles of different faculty members in methods of instruction and their organization of the learning environment?

☐ Are children encouraged to assess their own progress and monitor their own behavior?

Diagnosing Learning Needs

Before any teacher involves her children in open learning she should first make a careful assessment of their potential and their past experiences. This vital step is even more important in the open classroom than it is in the conventional setting because the success of the open approach depends largely upon the ability of the teacher to match her children to appropriate activities and materials. This diagnostic evaluation can be done at any time of the year, of course, but the best time for thorough inquiry is at the beginning of the school term. Children are always curious about their new teachers and new classrooms when they first attend the autumn session, and the open teacher should be equally curious about her young charges. ✔ One good suggestion is to set aside a week or two just prior to the opening of the fall session. During this time the teacher can invite to her classroom her newly assigned students for individual or small group informal activities that will help her to assess their background and their potential. Some of this diagnostic inquiry can take the form of games, puzzles, and other high-interest interactions or inventories (Figure 3). Late August or early September is also an appropriate time to take an extensive inventory of incoming children's interests and to review the collections of records maintained by the school.

✔ During the first few weeks of instruction the teacher is also wise to administer a variety of standardized tests, including those that suggest general achievement as well as those that indicate diagnostic possibilities. In fairness to the children several different measures should be used to give a fairly representative picture of their abilities. Many schools customarily devote time to testing at the outset of the instructional year. However, if such assessment is not scheduled, the open teacher may be able to acquire single copies of special tests by consulting the current issue of *Mental Measurements Yearbook,* the standard reference to all types of evaluation instruments. Use plastic overlays and self-checking techniques to show individual children how to take these tests during activity periods and how to summarize the results themselves.

✔ Another type of diagnostic device is the chapter or unit test that often accompanies basic textbooks in many subject areas. These can be administered by the students themselves. Given as a pretest they indicate how much knowledge each student already commands; individuals exhibiting a general mastery may be excused completely from certain units of study. The same test can also be employed as a posttest indicating how much progress a child has made in a specific area of study.

✔ There are several additional ways to discover useful information about children. One of these is the educational experiences inventory in which the pupil indicates the things he has already done both in school and outside (Figure 4). An aspirations checklist is used to suggest what a child might like to become or what he might like to participate in during school (Figure 5). A projective device allows the child to reveal more personal data in open-ended sentences (Figure 6). Another projective technique requires the child to respond to a set of titles assessing his wishful thinking (Figure 7). Helpful details are also produced by personal products such as an autobiography, a set of drawings such as self-portraits, pictures of friends, pets, and family, a booklet labeled "All About Me," or a scrapbook containing items of special interest.

Figure 3   Pupil Interest Inventory

1. Who are your favorite real-life heroes?
2. What are several television shows you like to see best?
3. Do you have a pet? If so, what kind is it, and what do you like and dislike about it?
4. What sports do you like to play?
5. Which sports do you like to watch?
6. What subject in school do you most enjoy?
7. In what subject are you most successful?
8. What kinds of books do you choose to read generally?
9. List several books you have read recently.
10. Who are your best friends?
11. What do you like to do after school?
12. What parts of the world do you like?
13. What organizations do you belong to in school?
14. What groups do you belong to outside school?
15. List any hobbies that you participate in.
16. Who are your favorite musical groups?
17. What jobs do you have to earn money?
18. What are the toys you like to play with most?
19. Which foods are your special favorites?
20. How do you spend your time during the summer?
21. What kinds of games do you play just for fun?
22. What is your favorite season of the year, and why?
23. Which holidays do you like the best?
24. What kinds of gifts do you especially appreciate?

Figure 4   Educational Experiences Inventory

1. Have you ever been on a long vacation trip? If so, where did you travel and what did you learn?

2. Have you ever fixed a machine? If so, what was it, and how did you do it?

3. Have you ever put on a play that you wrote yourself, or one that someone else invented?

4. Have you ever conducted a science experiment that was not required in school? If so, what did you discover?

5. Have you ever been to a museum? If so, with whom did you go and what did you enjoy the most?

6. Have you ever flown in an airplane, ridden on a train, or been on a large vessel? If so, where were you going?

7. Have you ever been camping? If so, where did you go and what did you like and dislike about it?

8. Have you ever lived on a farm or visited one? If so, what did you do every day?

9. Have you ever traveled to a foreign country? If so, how was it different from the United States?

10. Have you ever explored arts or crafts experiences outside school?

11. Have you ever learned to play a musical instrument or sing in a group?

12. Have you ever invented a mechanical device, either a real one or an imaginary one?

13. Have you ever composed an original poem or a song without being asked to do it?

Figure 5   Personal Goals Checklist

Please check which items you would like to be able to do some day.

- [ ] Doing well in art work
- [ ] Being able to read well
- [ ] Learning about people around the world
- [ ] Listening to people who disagree with me
- [ ] Playing a team sport really well
- [ ] Making friends easily
- [ ] Being elected the captain of a team
- [ ] Becoming a leader in class activities
- [ ] Being able to solve hard problems in mathematics
- [ ] Understanding scientific processes better
- [ ] Learning to speak some words in a foreign language
- [ ] Getting better control of my feelings
- [ ] Being more self-confident when speaking before a group
- [ ] Finding out about different careers that are open to me
- [ ] Learning how to play a musical instrument skillfully
- [ ] Being able to take suggestions better
- [ ] Learning how to control my temper
- [ ] Taking a greater share of responsibility in the classroom
- [ ] Discovering how to work with tools and mechanical devices
- [ ] Gaining better mastery of oral and written English
- [ ] Developing a greater creative sense
- [ ] Learning how to use standard reference works
- [ ] Growing a stronger and healthier body
- [ ] Expanding my interests in reading
- [ ] Finding out more about our community

Figure 6   Open Sentences Survey

Answer these unfinished sentences with the first thought you have.

When I grow up, I———
The best job in the world———
People think that I am———
Sometimes I get embarrassed when———
The worst thing about me is———
I would really like to change———
I feel there is nothing worse than———
Teachers generally make me feel———
You should know that my brother (sister)———
My parents are really———
I most enjoy———
I sometimes regret———
When people compliment me———
I really respect people who———
I get angry when———
I think I am good at———
My best friend sometimes———
I need help———
When I'm asked to help at home, I———
Getting up in the morning———
I feel uncertain of myself when———
I would like to know why———
When I'm asked to help someone, I———
My pet peeve is———
The prettiest thing———

Figure 7   Wishful Thinking Stories

Write a short composition on any of these topics.

If I Were President
If I Had a Million Dollars to Spend
The Things I Would Rescue in Case of a Fire
The Best Day in My Life
If I Could Start Life All Over
If I Could Turn into an Animal
Some Books to Take Along to a Desert Island
Things I Would Change About My Family
If I Had Three Wishes
If I Had a Magic Wand
The Most Needed Labor-Saving Device
The Ideal Child
The Perfect Friend for Me
The One Thing Most in Need of Change
A Dream Come True
My Most Satisfying Moment
Things That Make Me Proud
If I Had a Magic Carpet
Turning Me into Superman
My Favorite Daydreams
Writing the World's Greatest Story
The Wildest Nightmares
A Secret I've Never Shared
What a Teacher Ought To Be
A Notable Invention

chapter six
Openness Applied to Subject Areas

A New Approach to the Curriculum

A curriculum provides the overall plan outlining the objectives of an instructional program, and it suggests the ways in which these goals may be attained in classrooms. In a traditional school the curriculum is generally developed by the members of the faculty and tends to reflect their concern for conserving what has been historically significant in school instruction and for identifying what skills, concepts, and information ought to be transmitted from one generation to the next. In addition, the curriculum in traditional schools usually suggests the sequence in which learning should occur and the types of evaluation best suited to assess progress in each area of study.

In the open classroom the curriculum is developed differently. The teacher is aware of her obligations to the community and to society at large, for all children need to know certain basics; the ability to count, to read, and to spell are all timely and timeless intellectual skills. However, the open teacher does not feel bound to cover certain prescribed materials, nor does she believe that all students should be exposed equally to every area of study. The open teacher, while fulfilling her responsibility to communal needs, is equally responsive to children's individual needs, and she is alert to the potential for learning that is built into situations that arise during the day. She does not adhere to a predetermined order just for the sake of fulfilling someone else's expectations. She does not defer spontaneous discussions which reflect genuine and general pupil interest. This composite approach to curriculum matters not only guarantees a child reasonable contact with the skills and information that are essential as he develops into an effective citizen, but also personalizes instruction by retaining flexibility suited to individual abilities and to changing sets of circumstances in and about the classroom.

The open approach to curriculum also involves a concept referred to as "webbing," which allows students to move in several directions at the same time, to pursue different but related interests, to cross over subject matter boundaries, and to form different groupings for instruction. Webbing minimizes the one-dimensional movement of children so often found in conventional schools—an inexorable progression of skills beginning at the simple and becoming more complex, starting at the first page of a textbook and moving through it page by page. A visual demonstration of how webbing might work in a middle grades social studies unit, a unit on "Water," is represented in Figure 8.

The new flexible attitude is reflected in all areas of the curriculum; because open teachers are encouraged to adapt different subject areas, concepts, and methods to emergent needs, no two treatments of the curriculum will be quite the same. It is important, however, to describe briefly some possible characteristics of open curriculum in the classroom and possible operations of an instructional program in the major subjects.

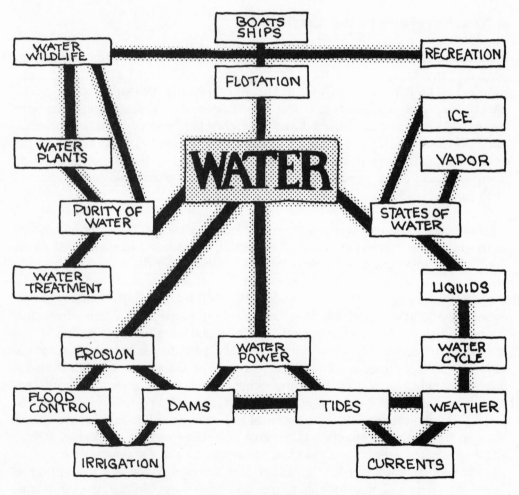

Figure 8   Example of "Webbing on Water"

Language Arts: Vehicle for Self-Expression

Since language is a primary means for expanding learning in the open classroom, language is not taught in isolation from the other subjects. The child sees the need to master communication skills because they enable him to find out the information he requires; he masters spelling, writing, and composition in order to convey clearly his discoveries to other people. Because the best way to become competent in language is to practice it in natural situations, the child learns not from a textbook as much as he learns simply by writing, talking, listening, and reading during the day. In this way the entire classroom becomes a language laboratory and every subject becomes a language class.

✔ In specific applications of openness to the curriculum, the child studying spelling, for example, chooses to learn words that are of value to him in his own personal writing, rather than to practice only a standard set of spelling words listed in the spelling book. He studies those words that he finds most difficult in his own composition exercises or that are of seasonal and personal interest; he quickly discovers that words he becomes excited about tend to become his for life. ✔ Further, the child sets his own personal spelling goals, rather than being bound to the inevitable twenty-words-per-week pace suggested by the textbooks. Some children may never be capable of twenty words a week, while other students may be motivated to progress far beyond this arbitrary limit. Some pupils may be excused entirely from the routine weekly testing that is an important part of conventional spelling instruction.

An example of openness in handwriting instruction arises during evaluation. Because the open approach assumes the importance of self-evaluation in all areas of the curriculum, the child practicing his penmanship is encouraged to assess his own progress. The teacher stresses general legibility, not an absolute standard of performance, and she emphasizes the need for communication in this, and all, language arts. ✔ The child examines each of his written products and identifies from time to time those letters, words and sentences that most closely approximate his own idea of legibility. He is encouraged to display the example of which he is most proud, and he continually compares present work with his past accomplishments. Each child maintains a collection of his written work which provides from month to month visible proof that progress is being made. His success is measured not in the endless rows of whorls and strokes on the penmanship paper, but rather in the letters, the stories, and the poems that have made meaningful his mastery of pencil and pen.

The open approach to oral and written composition is expressed in a degree of choice not usually found in the formal classroom. The traditional teacher tends to assign topics for all students at the same time. "What I Did on My Summer Vacation" is a typical example of the kind of assignment that bores children year after year and inhibits their spontaneity and creative sensitivities. ✔ The open teacher, though, encourages exploration of a greater variety of topics. Ones such as "At Home on Wheels," "Backyard Disasters," or "How to Talk to a Grizzly Bear" can describe interesting summer experiences, for instance. She also might suggest oral presentations or dramatic performances that represent the children's experiences.

In composition as in spelling the open teacher stresses the need for communication. However, she is not as concerned as is the traditional teacher about finding mistakes in usage or errors in spelling. She is aware that it is much too easy to mark mistakes with the red pencil and thereby destroy children's enthusiasm for writing. No child will be anxious to share his personal feelings if he knows the teacher is going to look at them only from the viewpoint of technical competency. ✔ In the open classroom each child is encouraged to write something every day. Most of this written work is not directly evaluated by the teacher, and it is shared with the class only if the author thinks it is worthwhile. The child's involvement in developing a class newspaper, in writing letters to his friends, or in preparing stories and poems for display in the school lobby not only shows him the elements of style he needs in his personal writing, but also demonstrates that an audience demands a greater degree of accuracy than a writer requires when he is composing for himself alone. This commitment to good performance becomes increasingly a personal responsibility, thereby releasing the teacher from countless hours spent correcting papers.

Personalized Reading

In the open setting the teacher sees to it that every child has a variety of reading matter from many different sources. The appropriateness of each item is determined through diagnostic investigation which begins with the first teacher-pupil contacts and continues throughout the school year. ✔ Instead of distributing to all children alike the same grade-level reading materials, the open teacher analyzes reading records, test results, interest surveys, and skills inventories, and decides not only what each child likes to read but also which of his reading skills require special practice. She then encourages each student to select those materials that are most interesting and most useful. This careful correlation between personal preference and learning media not only promotes the child's sense of responsibility in being able to choose his own learning activities, but it also helps him to feel more secure as he works in familiar territory with tasks that he can complete.

The teacher schedules reading activities so that each child can move at his own speed through a set of concepts or skills. Some children are entirely excused from grade-level programs, for there is no good reason why a student who is reading comfortably at the sixth grade level should read third-grade materials just because he happens to be in a third-grade classroom. Because children work at a personal pace in materials at different levels, reading does not become the race that it sometimes becomes in the conventional classroom. Each child may be using different materials at any given moment, so there is no opportunity or need to compare either the reading speed or the reading competency of any single child with that of any other child in the group. Whether or not a certain task is hard or easy is not discussed publicly, for each child works at a level which makes him most comfortable.

Individualizing Physical Education and Hygiene

One of the main responsibilities of the school is to teach children habits of personal hygiene, physical fitness, and safety awareness that will help them to maintain their strength, endurance, health, and security throughout their lives. However, the traditional fitness programs too often consist largely of mass calisthenics conducted without much regard for the individual capabilities of each pupil. The same exercises are prescribed for all members of the class, and the general fitness of each participant is assessed only by his score on a standardized test of physical abilities. Furthermore, the traditional approach to group physical activities emphasizes team sports, and the child who is neither athletically inclined nor interested in activities such as football, baseball, basketball, or track is not adequately served. The irony in such an approach is that the naturally endowed athlete rises to the top of the performance charts, and the most competitive person receives the plaudits of the instructor and the adulation of the peer group. By the same irony the children who need extra practice with specific skills are deprived of the necessary reinforcement because the teacher is preoccupied with identifying team captains and in developing even greater skills in those children who are already well muscled and well coordinated. And this is called physical education.

The physical educator who believes in the open approach challenges each child to establish his own performance goals. ✔ Each person maintains an individual and private record of his achievements in skills-related activities. These records may take the form of a chart or a graph that shows him his progress in different physical endeavors. ✔ Further, the open teacher, instead of assigning endless repetitions of set exercises, incorporates basic developmental skills as parts of games or movement experiences, the result of which is that the child develops overall stamina and muscle tone in an activity that is inherently interesting as well as helpful.

The open teacher is alert to the need for all students to respect each peer's achievement regardless of his ability because each person is a winner as he meets the goals he sets for himself. ✔ The sensible teacher is also alert to the social needs of students in physical training. No child is made the butt of ridicule by being the last child chosen every time sides for team activities are selected; instead, groups are randomly chosen, captains are identified by lot, and the varying abilities of the participants within each group are evenly employed. If competition rightly becomes a part of an activity, the teacher stresses the fun of the game. To emphasize individualization in open settings, the physical education instructor introduces personalized sports such as tennis, bowling, swimming, and jogging, fitness experiences that are likely to be continued in adult life.

✔ Another application of the open attitude toward fitness occurs as the teacher develops a stations approach in which a series of learning centers are set up in the gymnasium or on the playground. After students are instructed how to use safely each piece of equipment, every child is given an opportunity to explore fully the equipment. During a gym period, then, he is able to practice perhaps one or two skills intensively or else to have brief encounters with six or eight different ones. At each of these stations the teacher provides low-cost and no-cost equipment, much of which can be made by the students themselves from discarded materials. ✔ For example, by showing the class how to convert salvaged bleach jugs into colorful ball catchers, and by demonstrating the fun of tossing beanbags which students can make by filling and sewing shut ordinary garden gloves, the teacher not only encourages her children to recycle useful items but also encourages them to use those items informally during the remainder of the day as a relaxing break from the daily routine.

✔ In addition to general fitness activities like sports and games, movement exploration is a sound open approach to physical training principally because this mode of expression reinforces in the child the notion that experimentation and exploration are respected. Movement exploration combines both physical strength and grace, and it enhances the participant's sense of rhythm and dramatic delivery. The student, realizing that there is no single correct way to respond motorically to a piece of music, to the rhythm of a drum, or to a verbal stimulus, is allowed to solve each movement problem in his own unique way; the teacher presents situations, then encourages her students to suggest inventive solutions.

Instruction in health and safety can subscribe to the open approach's emphasis on respect for others by pointing out the need for social responsibility. The child who contracts a contagious disease may thoughtlessly expose others to the same discomfort. The person whose carelessness causes an accident not only suffers his own personal pain but also makes demands on the funds, time, and emotions of his parents and friends. In the same way that he records general fitness experiences, the child also checks his hygiene. No longer does the teacher conduct the morning health inspection; the child is not placed under pressure to report that he brushed his teeth, that he had a hearty breakfast, or that he scrubbed his hands and face before school. ✔ Instead, each member of the class maintains a personal log in which he records such details that comment on his own awareness of his growing body and his emerging sense of responsibility: his height, his weight, the foods eaten, the health practices followed, new levels of fitness, and good hygiene habits acquired.

Exploring Music and Art

The pupil-centered point of view that characterizes openness is also evident in music instruction to the extent that the teacher allows students to help determine the nature and the direction of their experiences. This principle is illustrated by as simple a matter as letting the class select most of the songs they prefer to use in vocal exercises or letting them choose the pieces they want to practice playing on instruments. If the prepared curriculum suggests certain specific skills or information that ought to be added to the children's musical background, the open teacher lets the pupils help to decide how this might best happen. In this joint determination of music content, activities, and materials, the open teacher once again notes what each child already knows, what he would like to learn, and what he is capable of performing. She includes the contemporary modes of musical expression along with the historical ones. She is as equally responsive to music from local radio shows as she is to music of the masters.

The open music class is not as tightly structured as are conventional music classes. During group instruction students may be seated informally about the classroom in comfortable positions or may even be moving in response to the music itself. The degree of class control depends on the ability of the teacher to capture children's desire to learn, to cultivate their feelings for music, and to help them respect the discipline that good music involves. In the open classroom musical experience also transcends the boundaries of time and schedules. The open teacher integrates music with all subjects in the curriculum, acknowledging the relationship between music, literature, and history, for example.

✔ Openness in music teaching also occurs through exploration of the medium. Music becomes a natural extension of other activities as children use voices and instruments to relax tensions or to stimulate their enthusiasm on a gloomy Monday morning. ✔ Students are encouraged to present informal performances for their age-mates and to entertain in the hallways or the cafeteria during breaks in the routine. ✔ They are also encouraged to invent new verses to songs they have learned, to make up original music, to develop their own instrumentation. Open music instruction also sensitizes the child's esthetic responses to the emotions evoked by the classics, the discipline required by the performer, the grace and strength of the dancer, and the creativity of the contemporary balladeer.

Art techniques in the open situation follow very closely those used in music experiences. Self-direction is present as the child is allowed to choose from many different media and as he examines their potential. Diversity and originality in products of art are stressed. ✔ The teacher refrains from distributing patterns of Santa Claus for all children to copy or fill with colors. Nor does she emphasize representational art, for it is more important that each child sets his own standard of performance. Only after many years of free expression does technical merit become important to the budding artist. In art as in music instruction, there is flexibility. Art materials are readily available for use during the day, either as equipment for a regular task at a predetermined time, as a means of tying together two or more subject areas, or as a way to interrupt the monotony of more routine involvements. The open teacher, who knows that art and music both are essential subjects for exploration, thinks of neither as a fringe or a frill to be taught only if there are time and money available. She is as concerned with her students' creative and esthetic potential as she is with their mastery of cognitive and physical skills.

Most important of all, the teacher respects beauty in everyday life. She provides for her youngsters many contacts with the immediate environment. ✔ She points out the color in the passing clouds, the intensity of thunder in a summer storm, the rainbow in an oil slick, and the pattern of shadows cast by a picket fence. She presents films, pictures, and records to supplement these firsthand encounters with the world. She presents art products that demonstrate the variety of interpretations expressed by craftsmen throughout history, and she shows her young charges that art is an important part of daily life by sharing her own interest in weaving, painting, and dance.

Making Social Studies Relevant

Open teaching makes the social sciences more meaningful through a notable approach to the study of comparative cultures. Whereas in the formal classroom the teacher tends to present conventional attitudes toward variations among peoples, treating differences with a touch of chauvinism and a sense of quaintness, and interpreting lifestyles which are different from the American way as somehow inferior, the open teacher points out that bamboo huts and a seaweed diet are just as logical for other peoples as ranch homes and hamburgers are for people in this country. The open teacher, while identifying such preferences, nevertheless indicates the need for variety and diversity, pointing out that individuality helps make life interesting and productive. She explains that the conventions chosen by one group of people, such as their mode of dress, their language, and their manner of living, are as appropriate for them as a different set of customs is for any other group.

Relevance in the open social studies program also occurs as the relationships between phenomena are made and parallels to the children's present experiences are drawn. The open teacher is not preoccupied with the memorization of masses of historical or geographical details. She is instead more interested in developing children's awareness of why certain countries produce certain goods. She points out the connections between historical events and current happenings, and she reinforces the notion that history is being made and recorded daily. ✔ She is less concerned with dates, places, and names and more concerned with lessons applicable to contemporary living. She presents figures from antiquity as real human beings who, like everyone else, suffered illnesses, worried about their bills, argued with their children and their colleagues, and, along the way, founded nations, wrote important documents, made scientific discoveries, and invented means to make life more useful and interesting.

Relevance is also apparent in open instruction as the child studying citizenship examines the roles and responsibilities of members of any social group. ✔ The open classroom serves as a model of a self-governing community. Each child in the class has his own functions to perform, representing an appropriate balance between his rights and his commitment to the needs of the minisociety. In his deliberations and discussions concerning rules and the governing of behavior, he learns to appreciate both the promises and the problems of the democratic process. He contributes to the general welfare of his classmates as he exhibits consideration for others' needs: doing his stint at cleaning up the clutter, waiting his turn in line at the drinking fountain, sharing his materials with his peers.

Self-Direction in Mathematics and Science

Pupil-centered instruction in these two curriculum areas features practices—such as the individual selection of study topics and apparatus—employed in the other subject areas. In addition, children can apply their skills in math and science problem solving to real situations. Children of all ages are filled with questions needing answers; curiosity is the hallmark of being young. When encouraging children to provide their own answers to their problems in the natural world, the teacher responds to children's questions by stimulating their own thinking. She is particularly pleased when her students provide insights and solutions that transcend her personal information and experiences. She is not worried about knowing all the technical data that children seek because she realizes that a timely "I don't know" can prompt her students to search further. Standard reference works and manipulative items are in constant demand in the math-science open learning centers.

One important outcome of self-guided inquiry is that the child attains a more objective outlook on life than he previously had. He learns to evaluate his own judgments and to question those persons whose information is based less on fact than on opinion. He respects the need to look at a situation from several different points of view and is not afraid to promote minority viewpoints if they can be supported with convincing evidence and logical arguments. Similarly, he is willing to reserve judgment when his collection of data is incomplete.

chapter seven
Setting Up Learning Centers

The learning center has become closely identified with the open school movement. Variously referred to as an activity center, an interest center, or a job center, the learning center is now a useful adjunct to openness because the child can find in it a collection of materials and media appropriate to his interests, a series of tasks and assignments that enable him to relate the equipment to his learning requirements, and a focus of attention that helps him to concentrate on a single concept while broadening his outlook on an entire field of study. It is important to note, however, that the philosophy of openness does not stand or fall solely on the teacher's ability to set up a series of interest centers in her classroom, for there are open classrooms where the materials, though convenient and multifaceted, are not arranged by theme or location. The crux of the matter is not the facility or the physical setting, but rather the freedom of opportunity presented the learner, and the variety of materials he is permitted to use. If learning centers are to be viable, however, there are several important elements to consider as they are organized.

Establishing Useful Criteria

✔ The first and most important consideration of setting up a learning center is that its functions be defined in behavioral terms insofar as it is possible to so describe them. Children should know the purpose of each piece of equipment and each activity that is a part of every learning center. They should realize that centers are not set up merely for random activity. They should be aware of each outcome built into the media and materials they are expected to use. The learning center should be perceived as a place where work is to occur, not as a place that serves as a reward of fun only for those few who happen to finish their other tasks early.

✔ A second important consideration is that learning centers should be largely self-operating. Materials should be readily accessible and self-explaining. The directions for the operation of machinery should be apparent and easy to follow. Procedures for completing learning activities should be clear and, when possible, expressed in programmed form. The methods of evaluation should be included as a part of any learning involvement.

The physical location, appearance, and management of each learning center should also be considered. ✔ Obviously, the noisy activities should be well separated from the quiet ones, and the messy experiences should not interfere with those that are tidy. Involvements that require a water source should be located close to a sink or a generous water container, and those that require easy access to other rooms or to the outdoors should be close to an exit. ✔ In some instances there is a need to limit the number of children at each station in order to guarantee adequate materials for each learner there. In the same manner, there may be a need to limit the amount of time children are to spend in one location. ✔ Rules for using each area should be posted on charts that catch the attention of the participants. Sources of further information should also be available. Each interest area should be as attractive and as comfortable as possible, soliciting children's curiosity and interest, and stimulating their efforts to learn.

✔ Another important organizational consideration is the notion of change. Many open teachers manage to have several learning centers operating simultaneously, but they do not leave any center on display any longer than it is needed to serve the children adequately. Some centers might well remain functioning for much or all of the school year. Other learning centers should be changed seasonally or topically to reflect the shifting moods and requirements of the class members. In this regard it is important not to change a center too often, for each child should have an adequate opportunity to use the center to his best advantage, and it should not present a bewildering variety of materials or an overwhelming selection of possible choices of activities. ✔ However, it is generally better to remove a certain learning center from the classroom while the interest remains high rather than to leave it until it has long outgrown its appeal. ✔ Sometimes it is appropriate to reintroduce certain learning centers later in the school year, or even to provide a place where the children themselves can collect personal learning materials and can develop skills and concepts for their classmates to explore.

✔ A final consideration for the learning center is variety. In the open classroom all types of media are appropriate. It is therefore essential to include in the center paper and pencil activities along with those that require record players and cassettes. Workbooks should be balanced with films and slides. Programmed items should be just as available as textbooks and library books. Manipulative devices are needed to complement those that are abstractly and verbally applied. All levels of competency should be liberally represented in the materials, and to accommodate all modalities there should be pictures and diagrams for children with visual preference in learning style, oral-aural opportunities for students more responsive to auditory stimuli, and tactile and kinesthetic involvements for those persons who receive their cues through their hands and bodies.

Providing Adequate Materials

Materials are obviously the key ingredient in a learning center, for without an adequate supply the learner cannot efficiently invest his time. Providing such a flood of materials can be a problem even in the best of circumstances, for budgetary restrictions are always a problem and no responsible teacher ever seems to have quite enough money for all her projects. The problem of supply is further compounded by the fact that the open teacher, in her commitment to individualizing her instructional program, has very little spare time for making her own learning aids. There are, however, several useful suggestions that make the job of providing materials slightly easier.

✔ The first proposal is to spend all presently available money more efficiently. For example, in the traditional reading program the teacher purchases for her children thirty copies of the same basal reader, thirty copies of the identical supplementary reader, and thirty copies of the same workbook. This investment may represent an expenditure of several hundred dollars—all of it geared to essentially the same learning experiences. Such a large amount of money is better redistributed by purchasing only a few single grade-level copies of the same materials—enough for a small group to use simultaneously if necessary—while spending the larger portion of funds for other related materials such as a subscription to a newspaper, a set of programmed materials, assorted titles from a collection of paperback books, some cassettes for listening, other trade books produced for different levels of reading ability, and any comparable items that satisfy the needs and interests of children in reading instruction. The same principle of diversified purchasing can be used in every other subject in the curriculum, so that small amounts of money are spent for limited sets of identical items, with the rest of the funds invested in permanent equipment and single copies of many other materials.

✔ A similar economy can be effected by changing workbooks and worksheets into permanent parts of the classroom collection, rather than having children use them as consumable materials. Since one of the key elements in self-directed learning is the matter of evaluation by the pupil himself, each child using a workbook or a worksheet can be shown how to place a piece of clear acetate over the answer blanks before responding to the questions. Using an erasable marking pen or pencil, he can write his answers on the protective overlay, then check his accuracy with the teacher's answer book. In this way many purchased consumable materials which are carefully handled can be used indefinitely.

✔ A third idea for extending the collection of learning center materials is to explore the possibilities of free and inexpensive media produced by businesses and industries, as well as by charitable and fraternal organizations. Perhaps the best source of information concerning this kind of learning aid is the series of books published by Educators Progress Service in Randolph, Wisconsin, which produces each year a set of ten or more different directories to free materials. Some of the titles in the series include

Educators' Guide to Free Tapes, Scripts and Transparencies

Educators' Guide to Free Guidance Materials

Educators' Guide to Free Social Studies Materials

Educators' Guide to Free Health, Physical Education and Recreation Materials

Educators' Guide to Free Curriculum Materials

Educators' Guide to Free Films and Filmstrips

The content of these resource books changes yearly although there is enough similarity from year to year to justify their biennial purchase—especially in view of the fact that each volume in the series costs more than $10.00. ✔ Many teachers find the single volume *Educators' Guide to Free Curriculum Materials* most useful of all the volumes published each year by the agency, and *Educators' Guide to Free Films and Filmstrips* also an outstanding investment for any school district. The quality of the materials produced by the sources listed in these guide books is outstanding and can do much to provide information on a wide variety of subjects of interest to both pupils and teachers. ✔ A similar source of information is the book *Free and Inexpensive Learning Materials,* which is produced by George Peabody College in Nashville, Tennessee. This book is updated every few years and has been retailing for several dollars. Here again, an entire school district's investment in just one copy of the source book could be well repaid many times over in free and inexpensive items that might be incorporated into the programs for learning centers in open classrooms.

✔ Another way to extend the usefulness of classroom materials is to purchase many that are open ended. Most learning aids should not be labeled for only one specific grade level because in any normal classroom there is a wide span of abilities represented. The kits produced by the Elementary Science Studies program are good examples of materials that stimulate good thinking and produce results regardless of the grade level at which they are used. The reading laboratories such as those prepared by Science Research Associates are other media that can be adapted to many different abilities and interests present in the room.

✔ An obvious method of diversifying learning materials is cooperative purchasing. If it is necessary to buy goods such as records, cassettes, and major pieces of reference material, for example, a teacher can combine budgets with at least one other open teacher in the same school to double or triple the variety of learning opportunities available. When such joint commitments are made it is important, of course, that the teachers select only those items whose quality will guarantee the greatest use by the largest number of children. ✔ If expensive resource materials are jointly bought, their use can be extended by placing them on wheeled carts to simplify their movement from room to room. ✔ Or it may be possible to place audio-visual equipment and reference materials in a hallway or a closet central to two or more classrooms. Converting the traditional library into a communal media center is another possibility.

Diversified materials for learning centers are also obtained by recycling discarded items. For example, many schools have extensive sets of discontinued textbooks that were superseded by the adoption of new series of texts in all subject areas. These old books are customarily either thrown out or sold for scrap. Instead of destroying or otherwise disposing of these books, it is feasible to cut them apart and use their pictures and written matter for many individual activities. Some books have complete sections dealing with a single topic: a science book, a social studies text, or a basal reader are samples of this. ✔ Remove the backs of these books and reassemble the useful sections in pamphlet form, each one with an attractive new cover made of cheerfully decorated tagboard. If illustrations and information in such books are outdated, suggest that the children use them as comparative sources of historical commentary on the way people formerly approached school topics. ✔ Or cut out the more interesting pictures, maps, and illustrations and use them to develop specific concepts. ✔ Use the one-page review questions at the end of chapters to stimulate further inquiry, and use the review problems to check proficiency. ✔ Cover single spelling activity pages with self-adhesive contact paper on which students can write with a felt-tip marker or grease pencil. Salvage individual lessons from other practice books and reassemble them in an attractive loose-leaf notebook. ✔ Collect back issues of commercially prepared student newspapers such as the *Weekly Reader* or the *Scholastic Press* periodicals for use as contemporary sources of information and current events.

Imaginative open teachers are also able to manufacture original learning aids from items on hand. Many devices that are otherwise available from commercial sources at considerable cost can be made easily from inexpensive materials that are readily available in most schools. ✔ To find examples of learning aids that can be replicated from discarded and secondhand materials, consult catalogs that are circulated by companies which produce commercial learning devices. There is no need, for instance, to purchase a simple mathematics game when the children are eager and capable of manufacturing their own from discarded fabric or recycled oilcloth or tagboard. A bodyboard for dramatic play is much more fun to use if the children themselves have fashioned it from cardboard rescued from a washing machine carton. ✔ Have the children find ways to adapt games and puzzles to the concepts and skills they are practicing; students are generally full of helpful ideas concerning how to make their own learning devices. ✔ In a corner of the classroom set up a "Fun Factory" for the purpose of converting found items into exciting and colorful learning aids. Outdated charts and posters are also appropriate for this application of inventiveness, along with local newspapers, comics, and cartoons. An ordinary road map has an obvious value in social studies or in mathematics, as have last year's calendars, old magazines, catalogs, and empty cartons.

✔ A similar source of valuable learning materials is the homes of the children themselves. Send home with the pupils lists of realia that are welcome additions to the classroom collection, either as outright donations or long-term loans. Sets of post cards, slides, pictures, souvenirs, and comparable items can be incorporated into the science and social studies centers, along with sets of fossils, shells, and plants. Even the "show and tell" activities so commonplace in the lower elementary grades are far more effective if children bring to these sessions items to share on a single topic, with the understanding that the materials are to be left in the classroom for further examination by students over a specified period of time. ✔ Encourage the children to share their hobbies and collections, and allow them to set up their own personal minicenters in which they can serve as the resident experts. ✔ Ask for the use of family games that are found in most homes. Checkers, Monopoly, Parcheesi, and ordinary playing cards can be adapted to many learning experiences. Toys illustrate principles in science and social studies. Donated children's books and reference works expand possibilities for learning.

✔ Add special interest to activity centers with materials procured at rummage sales, exchange sales, and auctions where it is possible to buy perfectly usable equipment, tools, and implements that enhance crafts instruction and simple construction projects. ✔ Explore antique shops for copies of old textbooks that illustrate both differences and similarities in the studies expected of children many years ago. ✔ Stimulate students' participation in subscriptions to book clubs and science clubs that not only provide at low cost interesting information for the individual subscribers but also provide an ample stock of supplementary materials for their classmates.

Using Large Areas Wisely

The open teacher utilizes work space in ways that are not generally found in the traditional classroom. For one thing, the open teacher expands study area beyond her own four walls and allows her children to use hallways, playgrounds, and other outdoor areas as a legitimate extension of the students' territory. ✔ Where there is ready access to the outside, you can set up interest centers that include play equipment, a water source, a play area, or a sand box. Such centers need not be confined to the preschool or primary grades, in which they are commonly found; instead, there are many concepts in science experiences of upper-grade students that can be served by such learning centers. Play equipment can be used, for example, to develop model communities as part of a social studies project. A "Green Thumb" garden center developed in part of the school grounds or donated by a sympathetic owner of neighboring property is an important adjunct of the classroom science program. A bird-feeding station and a weather station exemplify other types of student involvement in learning outdoors.

✔ In addition, it is possible to incorporate inside hallways as learning centers. In each open corridor attach to the walls fold-down shelves and use them for study carrels. When these shelves are not being used, flip them out of the way so that they will not impede the flow of traffic through the area. Also adapt hall windowsills, counters, and wall surfaces for displaying learning materials, student stories, and art work. Because local fire laws regulate the use of corridors, make sure that pieces of furniture or equipment do not clutter the passageway.

The open teacher also employs variety and flexibility in the way she furnishes her learning space. In conventional settings the pupils' desks are likely to be arranged in rows, but in the open classroom all furniture and equipment are subject to the specific needs of children, and as such its arrangement changes frequently during the year. The furnishings in open rooms may include different kinds of seating rather than uniform mass-produced pupil chairs and desks, and there may also be a variety of colors, textures, and designs. Some of the desks, chairs, and tables may come from commercial sources, but others may be salvaged from homes, rummage sales, and furniture stores. ✔ To serve the physical and psychological requirements of the students, however, any equipment should be adjustable, movable, and, when possible, multipurpose.

Before moving furniture about, consult the children, who will have many suggestions for its arrangement. ✔ Plan in miniature major shifts by using a graph-paper replica of the classroom and the large items contained in it. Mark with a bright color those permanent fixtures that cannot be readily shoved about. Then identify the items in each area that demand the greatest use or cause the heaviest flow of traffic. Doors, a drinking fountain, a water source, and a bathroom all help to determine the placement of individual locales for learning. Remember that there need no longer be a "back" or a "front" to the classroom; in fact the teacher's own work space may best be either centrally located in the room, within easy reach of each cluster of children and each interest center, or else completely off to one side of the room to allow the greatest space for the children in and about the center of the area.

Solving the problem of the too-small classroom is a challenge for the open teacher. In many older school buildings space is confining and the prospects for change are discouraging. One answer is to evaluate each major item in the classroom and to discard or place in storage elsewhere the more cumbersome and less functional furniture. ✔ Removing the large old-fashioned double-pedestal teacher's desk is one such possibility; transfer the most essential teacher materials to shelves in a closet instead and release the floor space for pupil use. ✔ Even a piano may be sacrificed or exchanged for an autoharp, an electronic organ, tone bells, a record player, or a guitar. ✔ Table space is rarely needed by all the students at the same time, so the number of tables may be drastically reduced.

✔ Similarly, not every child needs his own personal desk and chair. Instead, transfer their possessions to personal tote trays that are stacked out of the way when they are not in use. ✔ Make storage areas readily available to the children by removing doors from cabinets and closets, especially where such doors would swing out into the classroom.

Another way to economize indoor space in a small classroom is to use adaptable furniture. ✔ Certain types of chairs can be stacked in vertical arrangements. ✔ Wooden legs supporting tables can be trimmed several inches to allow one table to fit neatly underneath another table. ✔ Card tables can be quickly folded away when they are not needed. ✔ Utilize the empty space below the chalkboard rail by attaching with hinges a long wooden plank in such a way that it can be used as a table and folded down when more floor space is required. ✔ Acquire a set of magnets and convert the sides of a metal cabinet into an activity board or a display surface. ✔ Add casters to large pieces of furniture to facilitate moving them from place to place. ✔ Put those items most often used on wheeled carts. ✔ If tables are to be purchased, procure the type that is trapezoidal because these can be combined in many different arrangements to serve small groups. ✔ If there is volunteer help from parents or other aides, make tables from sheets of plywood, adding screw-on legs to permit the tables to be dismantled if it becomes necessary. Design such homemade tables so they can be nested at the end of the day. ✔ Salvage discarded window shades and convert them into permanent charts that can be rolled up when not in use. ✔ Contact storage and moving companies for slightly damaged wooden crates and heavy reinforced cardboard containers; use these as tables and chairs during the day and turn them over to be filled with toys, games, and other learning materials as the children leave. ✔ Use planks for work benches, balance boards, or partitions. ✔ Make study centers of cardboard panels that can be laced together and later dismantled.

Adding another level of floor space is still another approach to the utilization of the classroom. ✔ Raised platforms and stacks of individual cubicles are two possibilities. Platforms can be made by tying together the legs of tables and padding the surface of the tables with carpeting or a rug. Children can then be allowed to study on the top surface as well as in the "cubby" underneath. ✔ If the raised platforms are large enough, add individual cubicles by salvaging from appliance stores a set of large cardboard cartons; paint these cartons attractively and let the children use them as private spots to read, to listen to a record, to write a story, or to review a skill. Cut interesting openings in these boxes and attach imaginative labels or street addresses for even greater enjoyment. Cut the top and bottom flaps from these cartons so they can be folded away when they lose their appeal (Figure 9). ✔ Additional levels of work spaces can be made by acquiring from a secondhand furniture store a sturdy wooden bunk bed; with paint and decals convert this item into a two-story reading center for several students to use simultaneously.

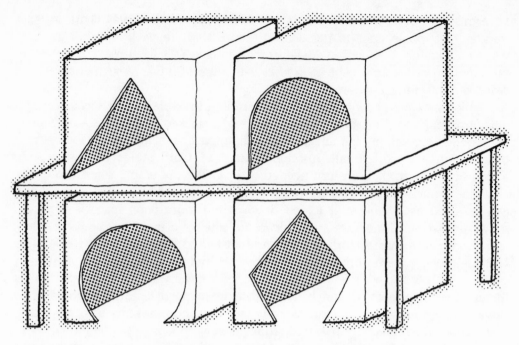

Figure 9   Multilevel Study Carrel

When open teachers establish learning centers, the classroom is often sub-divided into sections, each of which has its own particular appeal to students, some areas serving as study centers for groups and others serving as individual project areas. It is helpful to set up partitions and room dividers that not only control the flow of traffic in the classroom but also make the entire environment more colorful and attractive. Several kinds of dividers are useful for this purpose.

- Attach a coarse-meshed fish net from the ceiling, attaching to it objects that relate to the sea.
- Connect a series of discarded styrofoam or paper cups into a cascade of color suspended from the ceiling on lengths of yarn.
- Suspend from the ceiling varying strands of roving, yarn, beading, crepe paper streamers, or cording obtained at a drapery shop.
- Salvage plastic flowers and wire them together to cover sections of chicken wire or hardware cloth.
- Have the children make gay paper chains from colored paper or shiny foil.
- Collect a group of house plants and arrange them in a set of macramé hangings, or make an array of plants on a free-standing shelf.

✔ Utilize discarded wooden window screens. Paint and repair them, as needed. Decorate them with children's embroidery done with yarn and string threaded through the screening itself. Attach two or more screens together with hinges so they will support themselves in the room.

✔ Drape long swaths of unbleached muslin with block-printing decorations by the pupils.

✔ Section off a learning center for science with a shower curtain that is decorated with fish, shells, and other motifs of the sea.

✔ Attach to light fixtures long strips of mural paper or adding machine tape gaily painted by the students.

✔ Connect panels of stiff cardboard with fabric tape or masking tape. Make them tall enough to stand by themselves. Arrange these panels into hexagons or other polygons of floor space. Cut geometric shapes into each one to allow closer supervision.

✔ Set up stacks of sturdy cardboard boxes, each surface serving as a display area.

✔ Staple together sections of pastel styrofoam egg cartons and hang them from light fixtures.

✔ Make a privacy wall by stuffing newspapers into oatmeal boxes, shoeboxes, cereal boxes, or other cartons, then stacking them.

✔ Erect a large loomlike device on which children can weave strips of colorful fabric, yarn, strips of paper, grasses, and other objects from nature.

✔ Set up a number of large compartmented boxes often discarded by liquor stores. Arrange these boxes on their sides in a vertical display and use the compartments for storage.

✔ Direct the flow of traffic from one center to another by affixing a set of colorful self-adhesive footprints to the floor, or by applying bright arrows or replicas of the human hand to wall surfaces.

✔ Make a type of bead chain suspended from the ceiling by interlocking the metal pop-top openers salvaged from soft drink dispensers.

✔ Hang from the ceiling large numerals, letters, signs, and other topical items to direct children to their appropriate work stations.

Arranging Personal Study Spots

In addition to setting aside larger portions of the classroom for different group related learning centers, the open teacher is also responsible for designating small spaces where individual children can engage in personal investigation and thought. To accommodate these individual needs, consider some of these possibilities.

- Make an Indian teepee from long strips of wood or bamboo and cover the construction with transparent plastic sold at hardware stores, lumber yards, or farm supply markets. Ask the children to embellish each panel of the teepee with tribal designs.

- Use an old beach umbrella or patio umbrella to shelter a small oval reading rug. Add several soft toys or a comfortable cushion.

- Place a blanket inside a large oval laundry basket, or make a large beanbag stuffed with styrofoam fragments or scraps of foam rubber.

- Salvage large truck or tractor inner tubes. Inflate the tubes and fill the inner circle with a large round cushion.

- Recycle a fiber drum discarded by a commercial bakery or laundry. Place it on its side and block it with cushions to keep it from rolling, or stand it up and cut interesting shapes into the sides for entrances and windows (Figure 10).

- Cut apart large panels of cardboard cartons and incise slots into these with a sharp knife in such a way that they may be assembled slot-to-slot somewhat like the toy "Lincoln Logs."

- Lay on its side a large refrigerator carton and use it for a private viewing room for filmstrips. Or set it on end for a book house. Cut a door in the side and decorate the interior with wallpaper samples contributed by a local paint or furniture store (Figure 11).

- Throw a blanket or a scrap of canvas over a short stepladder, a pair of sawhorses, or an easel.

- Cover a card table with a remnant of colorful fabric, plastic, or oilcloth.

- Use cardboard boxes or pieces of cardboard cartons to subdivide study space or to set up personal learning centers (Figures 12, 13).

- Borrow a pop-up tent for a cozy spot for study. The interior supports of such a tent permit it to stand without pegs. Make a substitute tent with a rectangle of canvas thrown over a length of rope drawn between two hooks.

- Erect rolls of colorful corrugated cardboard to make free-form study carrels in different parts of the classroom.

- Salvage sheets of pegboard and connect them with wires to make L-shaped study points that will stand on the floor without any other support.

KC

KID
CASTLE

Figure 10   Cardboard or Fiber Drum Kiosk Carrel

Figure 11   Refrigerator Carton Study Booth

A. REFRIGERATOR CARTON OBSERVATORY

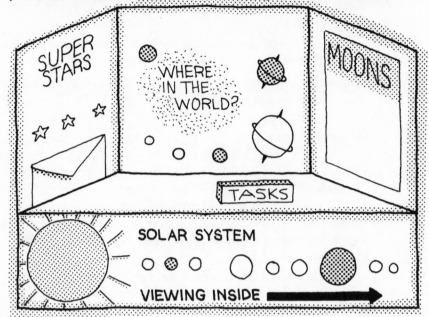

B. BOX-ON-TABLE REFERENCE CENTER

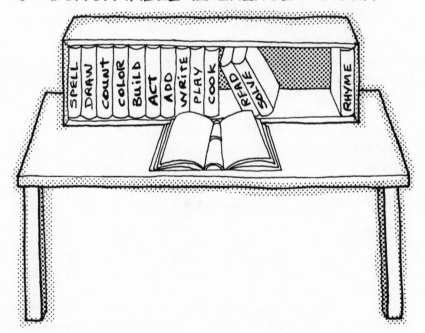

Figure 12   Observatory and Reference Center

- Change a large appliance carton into a houselike container by cutting the top panels into triangles that can be laced together to make a pyramidal roof.

- Purchase a new plastic garbage can and lay it on its side for a rest stop or a reading spot.

- Transform a large cardboard box into a good individual work station by cutting it apart and placing it on the top of a table. Use the flaps of the box as instructional displays for each study spot.

- Add interest to table-top study centers by designating certain types of inquiry for each one. Decorate and arrange a series of cartons on several tables and label each box with a name indicating its function in the classroom "community." For example, the "Garage" might contain information relating to simple machines; the "Grocery" might present experiences concerning diet and nutrition; the "Bank" is the obvious location for mathematical devices and activities; the "Library" houses the book and story materials; and the "Studio" makes available the media required for involvement with arts and crafts. Encourage the children to decorate the cartons in keeping with the theme of each one, and store in them directions for different tasks as well as the materials needed in fulfilling the tasks. Convert the flaps of the boxes into attractive billboards enticing the children to get involved in each "store."

- When individual spots have been arranged, give them all distinctive names to further attract children to their use: "The Chatter Box," an acoustically treated compartment for two children to use in sharing information or in studying for a mastery test; a "Truth Booth" filled with standard reference materials, such as a dictionary, a set of encyclopedias, and an atlas; a "Look Nook" for viewing filmstrips or film loops; a "Chuckle Hutch" covered and filled with colored Sunday comic sections, cartoons, jokes, and riddles, the "Art Park" for painting and crafts.

Making Self-Checking Learning Aids

The programmed instructional approach has been used by many schools for more than a decade, but it is in the open classroom that pupil-checked materials and media are particularly appropriate. Self-pacing and self-evaluation are important elements of self-directed situations, and by using self-checking items a child can have immediate reinforcement of the accuracy of his responses and the adequacy of his understandings. Rather than having to wait for help from the teacher, he can find out firsthand whether or not he is proceeding correctly. This immediate reinforcement obviates the need to unlearn wrong impressions and relearn faulty in-

A. CARDBOARD CARTON STUDY CARRELS

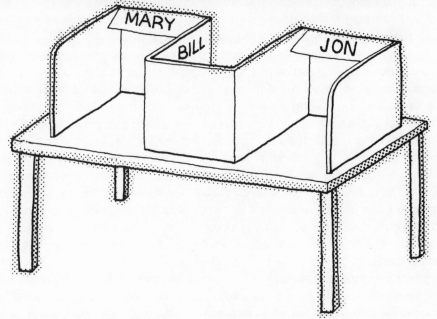

B. FOLDED CARDBOARD SUBJECT CENTERS

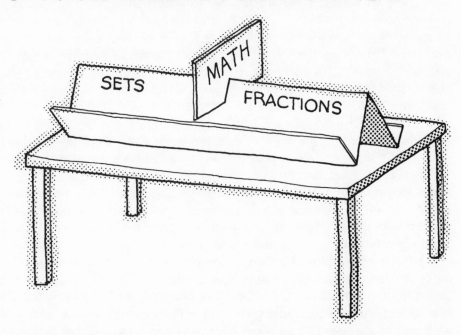

Figure 13   Study Carrels and Subject Centers

formation. Anyone who has observed in traditional classrooms the many papers and workbooks stacked and unchecked on the teacher's desk at the end of the day cannot help but wonder how many errors and misunderstandings some children took home with them as they left the school.

The open teacher's expectation that the child will proceed at his own speed and will evaluate his own responses requires that she trust the ability of the child to handle the chore. Most students can do this job honestly and fairly without cheating or without borrowing answers if they are charged with the responsibility from the outset of their educations. Because in the open setting the element of competition is minimized and open learners are frequently not working in the same materials at the same time, there is no need to cheat. Each child finds it more challenging to compete against himself rather than against the performance of his peers. The teacher recognizes each child's best efforts, so there is no rush to be the first one done, nor is there pressure to become the very best achiever in the room. In the open classroom the teacher does not point out individual students as examples for other children to emulate, and very little attention is paid to grades on report cards, even if they are required as a part of the school policy. Under such ideal circumstances, cheating on programmed materials is not likely to occur. In the rare instances when a child does not do his self-checking honestly, he needs only to be gently and privately reminded that other assessments will be made by the teacher, and that the pupil's inability to perform at a reasonable level of competency may prompt the teacher to ask him to repeat certain learning activities.

There are several fairly simple ways to enable students to check the accuracy of their own daily efforts. ✔ The simplest method of checking a paper-and-pencil activity is to give the pupil the answer book and allow him to correct his own work. You might want to tear out and laminate answer sheets found in teachers' manuals; this treatment provides wider distribution of answer sheets and also insures longer wear. Number answer sheets with large numerals and color code them by topic or by unit. Arrange them in a loose-leaf notebook to facilitate their use. ✔ If worksheets made by you or another teacher are to be used, write the answers on the back of each page, or write them upside down at the bottom of the paper, asking each person to fold under the portion that contains the answers so that he can concentrate on the learning task rather than think about looking at the answers. ✔ Children checking their own replies may be issued crayons to be used only for marking; select those markers whose colors contrast with the usual pencils, crayons, or pens that the students use in completing the worksheets, puzzles, and study papers.

✔ A simple electrical battery board can be constructed to serve a wide variety of self-checking activities that involve simple matching skills. Such a device can be made from thin sheets of hardboard or plywood, and is easily within the ability of a middle grade or an upper grade student to assemble as a school project. On each side of the board's face arrange either a vertical row of hooks, card pockets, or other compartments to allow for easy changing of the stimulus questions and their appropriate responses. The frequent rearranging of questions and answers prevents the children from merely memorizing the patterns of the matching elements. Brass fasteners, bell wire, and a dry cell are the main pieces required for the battery board, along with a buzzer or lights that signal the correct answer.

✔ An unusual self-checking device is made from a discarded plastic jug and is useful for many different single-answer tasks in the curriculum. Cut a slot in the side of the jug close to its bottom and parallel to the bottom in such a way that the slot will hold a small packet of stimulus cards when the jug is laid or held horizontally. Write a problem at the top of each card; and on the bottom of that card write the correct answer to the query. The child holds the handle of the jug horizontally in such a way that he can see only the stimulus question at the top of each card. When he thinks he knows the answer, he peers through the open neck of the jug, and in so doing he is able to see the answer on the bottom of the card. If necessary, cut additional holes or slots elsewhere in the side of the jug to allow sufficient light for the child to see clearly the hidden portions of the task cards (Figure 14).

✔ When a series of questions is a part of individual reading activities, attach to the front inside cover of each book one or more library card pockets. In each pocket place index cards on which the questions are posed. As the child reads the book he may refer to the questions from time to time to guide his search for the appropriate information. On the back cover of each book also place library

Figure 14   Bleach Jug Viewer

card pockets in which the answer cards are placed, each question number cued to the appropriate response. Use different colored index cards to further differentiate between questions and answers.

✔ Use a circular pizza board or any other round piece of cardboard to fashion a clothespin wheel for simple matching experiences. On the back of spring-type clothespins place a small dab of paint or a tiny piece of colored fabric tape; on the back of the wheel place a spot of color that matches the one on the back of each clothespin. On the front the wheel place a series of questions, each one written in a different section of the wheel that has been divided to resemble a cut pie. On the front of each clothespin write an answer to one of the various questions on the wheel. When the child has examined all the questions on the face of the wheel, and has placed in position all the matching clothespins, he can turn the board over and quickly see if his answers are right simply by checking to see if the color spots match (Figure 15).

✔ Large rectangles of cardboard can be cut to fit exactly over the worksheets that students are checking. When multiple choices are available, cut out windows in the tagboard to coincide with the placement of the correct replies on the student paper. The child can use a crayon or other marker to indicate those responses that appear in the appropriate windows (Figure 16). ✔ A variation of this cut-out overlay is to have a series of single-answer questions, such as additional problems, on one side of the tagboard. Cut out horizontal slots in the tagboard just wide enough to allow the child to write his solutions to the problems on his own paper placed underneath the overlay. When the child has finished working the computations he merely turns over the tagboard overlay, and on the back, in proper sequence, are the correct solutions to his problems (Figure 17).

✔ Make a dowel rod sorter from a cardboard box about the size of one that is used to hold recipes or envelopes. Cut a packet of stimulus cards to the same size as the box, allowing the packet to fit comfortably inside it. Through the bottom of each stimulus card punch holes that match in alignment the positions of similar holes poked through the bottom of the front of the box. Make all these holes uniform and large enough to accommodate a small dowel rod. At the top of each card write a simple question, and directly underneath the question write several possible responses, only one of which is correct. Under the correct answer at the bottom of the card, cut away the punched hole in such a way that when the child inserts his rod through the correct hole in the side of the box, the cut-away portion will enable him to lift out the card and place it at the rear of the packet. However, if the child chooses the incorrect solution to the problem, he will not be able to pull the card from the box because the rod inserted through the hole will hold it down (Figure 18).

✔ Another version of the programmed box is the flipper box in which the packet of stimulus-response cards is inserted from the side position. In this exercise, however, there are two possible answers randomly ordered on the bottom of

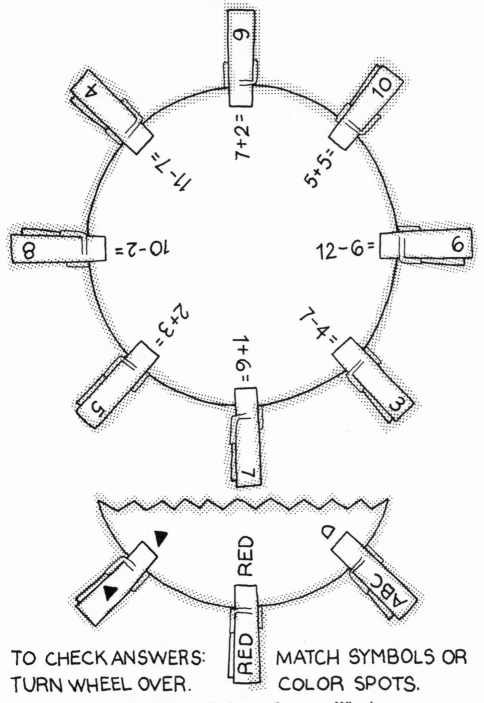

TO CHECK ANSWERS: MATCH SYMBOLS OR
TURN WHEEL OVER.   COLOR SPOTS.

Figure 15   Clothespin Learning Wheel

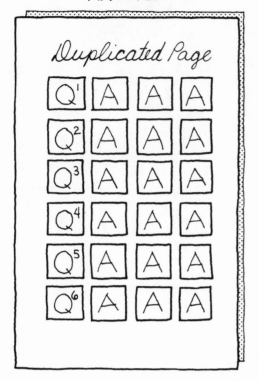

PUT X ON CORRECT
ANSWER

Duplicated Page

Q¹ A A A
Q² A A A
Q³ A A A
Q⁴ A A A
Q⁵ A A A
Q⁶ A A A

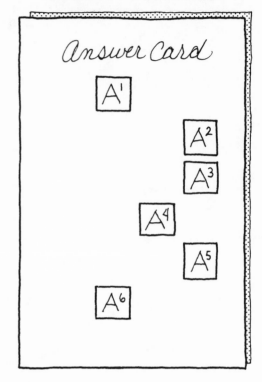

COVER PAPER WITH CARD
CHECK YOUR CARD

Answer Card

A¹
A²
A³
A⁴
A⁵
A⁶

Figure 16   Overlay Checker

each card. Underneath the large window where the questions appear there are two smaller windows where the two possible answers are written. Beside each response is a small cardboard flipper that can be lifted. Underneath one flipper is the word "yes" and underneath the other flipper is the word "no." By folding back a flipper the child can see which of his two choices is the correct one (Figure 19).

✔ For a series of simple recognition skills make "lift-up" charts (Figure 20); or make a lift-up checker by folding a piece of paper in half lengthwise and cutting slits in one side so there are three or four flaps for the child to lift. Write a simple question on each flap and challenge the pupil to lift the flap to determine if he has thought of the correct answer (Figure 21).

✔ Make self-correcting sequence cards for learning situations in which a series of items must be placed in a proper order: the main points in the outline of a story; words in an alphabetizing drill; the main events in a historical period; an ascending order of numerals. In each case, place every element of the multi-part task on a separate card. On the back of each card in the series place a letter which, when all the cards are placed in correct sequence and then turned over,

WRITE YOUR ANSWERS ON SEPARATE PAPER

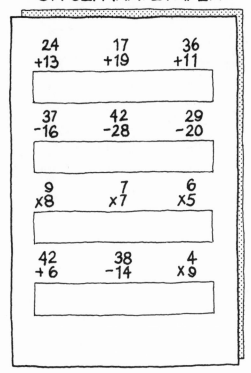

FLIP THE CARD AND CHECK ANSWERS

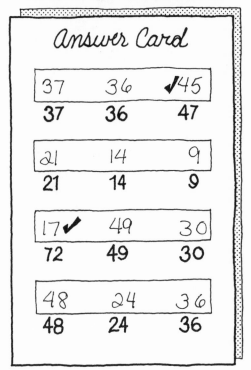

Figure 17   Overlay Checker

POKE ROD IN RIGHT HOLE, LIFT CARD OUT

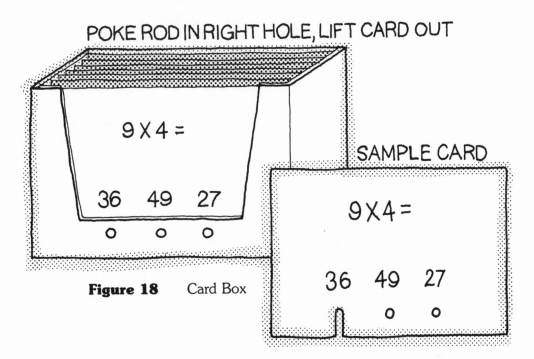

Figure 18   Card Box

Figure 19   Flipper Box

will spell a word of encouragement. If the child has placed the several elements of the task in the right sequence, by turning the cards over in position the correctly spelled word will indicate his success in the activity (Figure 22).

✔ Children have worked with self-checking flash cards for years. One way to add interest to these basic devices is to cut them into seasonal shapes such as valentines, pumpkins, or stars. Pairs of students can take turns giving and checking answers.   ✔ Cut out a large shape resembling an animal or cartoon face. Around the perimeter of the face write a series of simple queries, and beside each one punch a hole just large enough for a pencil to fit. On the reverse side of the face beside each hole write the correct response. Working in pairs, children can check their proficiency, one poking his pencil through the hole while he answers and his partner seeing if his answer is right (Figure 23).

✔ Using slider strips any simple worksheet can be converted into a programmed item simply by leaving a margin on either side to record the answers. Such a margin can be folded back while the student is working the problems.

✔ Another way to help children evaluate their work is to provide a tape recorder at each interest center. Individual cassettes can be used to record instructions for an activity, to record the students' responses to his tasks, and to provide the correct answers once the activities are done. To make the machine easier to use, place a piece of green fabric tape on the "Play" button and a comparable

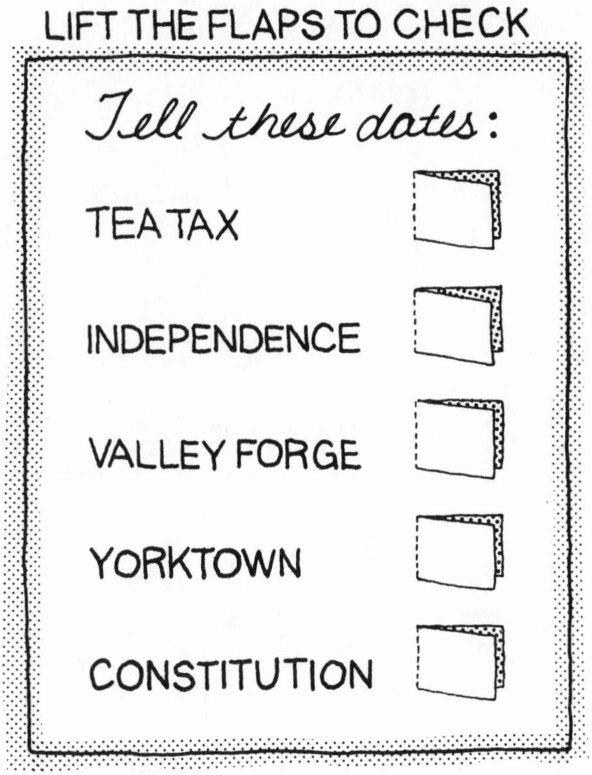

LIFT THE FLAPS TO CHECK

Tell these dates:

TEA TAX

INDEPENDENCE

VALLEY FORGE

YORKTOWN

CONSTITUTION

Figure 20   Lift-Up Chart

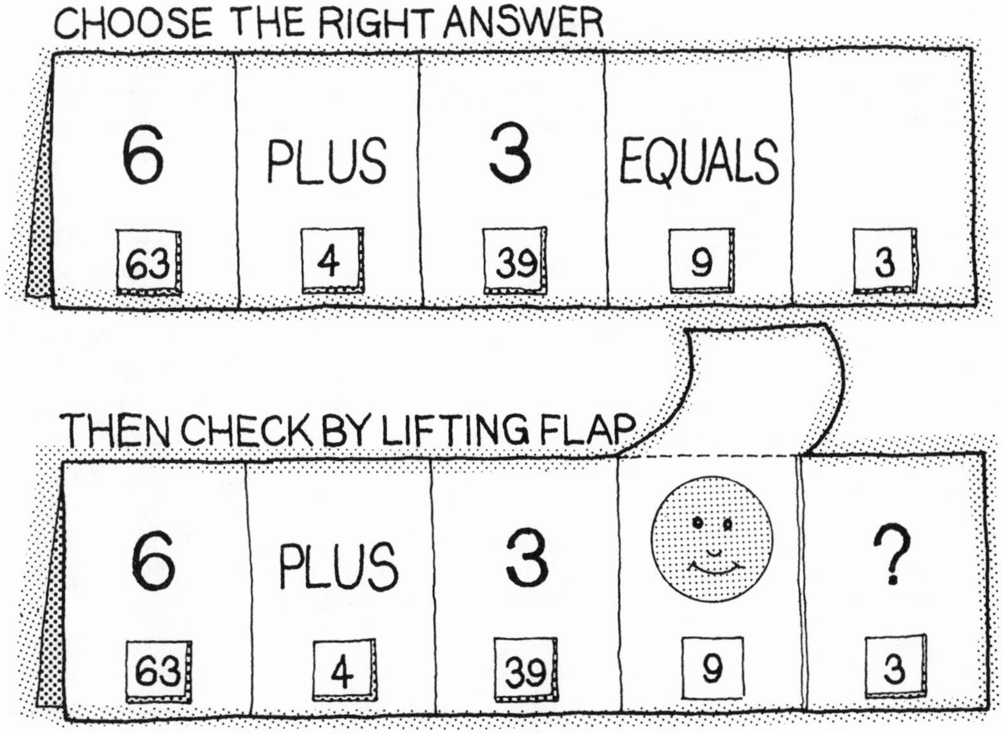

CHOOSE THE RIGHT ANSWER

6   PLUS   3   EQUALS

63   4   39   9   3

THEN CHECK BY LIFTING FLAP

6   PLUS   3   ☺   ?

63   4   39   9   3

Figure 21   Lift-Up Checker

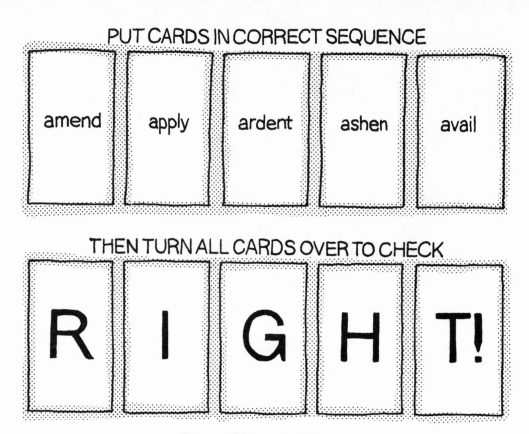

Figure 22   Card Array

piece of red tape on the "Stop" button. Place a yellow warning label on the "Record" button to prevent the children from accidentally erasing the taped materials.

✔ Puzzle pieces are helpful in simple self-checking activities. On pieces of cardboard or tagboard write both the question and its answer. Then cut apart the two matching elements in such a unique way that the appropriate elements can only join each other, not any unrelated question or answer. If the child chooses the wrong answer, the puzzle will not fit together. Adapt this same approach to items that must be placed in sequence: numerical information, alphabetical tasks, chronological events. Once again, the child's ability to place the items in correct order will be verified by the fit of the puzzle pieces (Figure 24).   ✔ A simple self-correcting spelling puzzle is made by drawing a picture of the object to be spelled with the word correctly spelled at the bottom of the picture. The picture is then cut apart into vertical strips which are mixed up. The child spells the word by reassembling both the word and the elements of the picture that illustrates it (Figure 25).

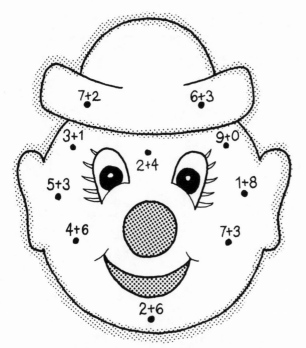

POKE PENCIL THROUGH HOLE
FLIP FACE OVER TO CHECK

Figure 23   Poke Checker

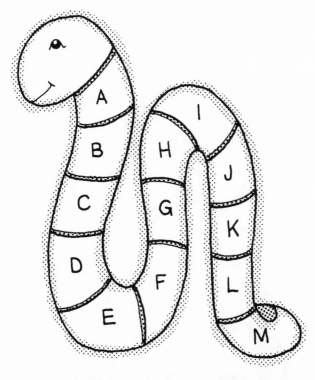

Figure 24
Self-Checking Sequence Puzzle

LETTER STRIPS SPELL WORD; ASSEMBLED PICTURE CHECKS IT

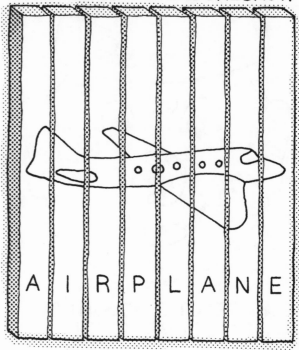

Figure 25
Spelling Checker

PULL RING ON YARN; MATCHING RING MOVES

The Right Ring!

9-4 =   8

17-9 =   1

3+7=   10

6-5 =   5

4+3 =   12

8+4 =   7

Figure 26
Ring Checker

✔ A pull-ring device is a chart on which strands of yarn connect each question with its appropriate answer. A tug on one ring moves the other one (Figure 26).

Developing Pupil Contracts

The student contract is essentially an agreement negotiated between the pupil and the teacher in which certain studies and their accompanying procedures may be stipulated by either party. In the open classroom the children are deeply involved in making many of the decisions concerning their learning experiences, and the degree of participation in setting up and fulfilling the contract reflects the ability of each student to handle the responsibility. Ideally the contract allows the child to set his own goals, to select his own materials, to schedule his own time, and to evaluate his success. However, some children are less capable or less interested in taking the initiative in these matters; but even they should be permitted to make agreements concerning the order in which their work is to be done, the time of day in which selected activities may be attempted, or the kind of materials and media to be used in their learning (Figure 27).

One type of pupil contract is based on the assumption that the teacher will control the vertical movement of children through a sequential series of skills, but that the child is responsible for his horizontal development as he selects at any point in the instructional program reinforcing activities from a broad array of media and materials that are equally difficult for him. For example, the teacher might direct the child's progress through a basal reader, but the child himself might choose from several supplementary readers or other materials to buttress his reading skills at a designated level of difficulty.

A contract may also be drawn up between the teacher and the class as a whole. The entire group, setting a goal for achievement in a selected area of the curriculum, might decide to learn the spelling of a certain number of words during a week or a month, to raise their cumulative average in reading test scores one full grade level over the course of the year, or to read a predetermined number of library books during a grading period. A group contract may also be established to define objectives for classroom behavior; in exchange for good conduct there may be a stipulation of a tangible reward provided by the teacher.

Just as there are several kinds of contracts, there are also a number of elements that might be included in them. Remember, of course, that not all items necessarily should appear in any given agreement.

✔ Identify the purpose of the activity. State the specific educational objectives that you expect to be reached. State these objectives in such a way that the child can easily participate in the assessment after he is done.

✔ Describe the medium to be used, and detail the place and the circumstances under which the learning is to occur. Detail conditions such as the

*Must Do	MON.	TUE.	WED.	THU.	FRI.
MATH	* p.63		* p.64		* p.65
READING	*phonics	*puzzle	*story	*p. 16 →	*25
WRITING	*rewrite →	*→		*poem	
SCIENCE		* pets		* pets	
ART - SOC. ST.					
MUSIC					
FITNESS					
CONSTRUCTION					
HEALTH					
SPELLING	*pretest		*games		*test
LISTENING					
DRAMATICS					

NAME: David

WEEK OF: Feb. 9

Others:

Share postcard collection

Figure 27   Individual Contract

learning center or the area of the room, the number of children who may be engaged in the same activity at the same time, and the controls required for use of equipment.

✔ Include the amount and the duration of time. Some contracts may be long-term agreements, and others may involve planning for a single subject or a single day.

✔ Deal with the level of proficiency expected. Some tasks might call for complete mastery, as, for instance, "Spell all ten words on the list correctly." Other contracts might specify a more general level of competency: "Work correctly any seven problems listed on this page," or "Use this art medium for at least ten minutes, stopping when you feel you have a good idea of its possibilities."

✔ Provide for the means of the evaluation and the person who is to do the assessment. This in most instances might include some type of self-checking. Sometimes the evaluation might be done by a partner or by the teacher herself.

✔ Determine the reward to be offered. Usually the child's satisfactory completion of the learning activity is adequate recompense. However in many schools where open classrooms operate there is still a requirement that some type of letter grade or numeral grade be computed and reported. If a report card is still mandatory, set up a contract on a point system with grades awarded for categories of points earned: "Accumulate any combination of 20 points on these projects for a 'D'; 40 points earns a 'C'; 60 points will give you a 'B'; 60 points plus 10 bonus points is an 'A' " (Figure 28).

Figure 28 Social Studies Contract

Unit: "The American Revolution"

Choose any combination of projects that equal these grades:

"A" = 65 points   "B" = 50 points   "C" = 35 points

(Bonus points will be given, in addition, for extra effort, special insights, or unusual artistry.)

Paint a mural on any topic: 1775 to 1783	(5 pts.)
Prepare a research report using three different sources	(8 pts.)
Interview a local history expert	(3 pts.)
Make a booklet of original pictures	(5 pts.)
Prepare a poster recruiting the Continental Army	(5 pts.)
Make a chart showing the resources of both sides	(5 pts.)
Set up a large map of at least ten major battles	(5 pts.)
Build a model of John Paul Jones' ship	(8 pts.)
Display a collection of bicentennial realia	(5 pts.)
Survey any ten adults concerning the colonists' claims	(8 pts.)
View any three filmstrips and respond to the task cards	(5 pts.)
Listen to the record "Songs of Liberty"	(2 pts.)
Play an original song, or sing one, about the period	(3 pts.)
Post a bulletin board display	(7 pts.)
Read a chapter in the text and take a test on it	(5 pts.)
Produce an original replica of the "Declaration"	(5 pts.)
Read a book of fiction about this period, plus one task card	(9 pts.)
Read a biography from this period, plus one task card	(9 pts.)

Write a five page diary of life during the War	(7 pts.)
Make and demonstrate one craft item from the period	(5 pts.)
Dress several dolls in the fashions of the time	(6 pts.)
Prepare samples of foods used in the colonies	(5 pts.)
Plan a diorama of house interiors	(8 pts.)
Build a model of Independence Hall	(9 pts.)

Using Charts and Posters

Charts and posters are especially useful in the open classroom because they not only present factual data to the learner but also help him to direct his own learning and to discover related resources and information. Charts in learning centers can show how many children are permitted in a given area at one time, and they can tell the students what the time limits are for using the center. A chart is also helpful in showing explanations of processes and in giving directions for the children to follow. Pictures or illustrations are especially appropriate to young children and to older students who have reading problems. A chart may also pose the principal questions that should be answered at a given learning center.

A topical chart is one which suggests a variety of subjects from which a child selects those studies of greatest interest or of greatest need. ✔ In a reading center, for example, use a chart listing fifty different book activities that would be suitable for students to pursue. ✔ At the art center display a chart that suggests ways for children to experiment with different media. Along one axis of the chart list all the possible art opportunities: crayon, tempera paint, cut paper, clay, chalk, and yarn are a few examples. Then along the other axis list some of the involvements: texture, light and dark, constructions, design, and patterns are several ideas. As the children work at the art center, encourage them to see how many different combinations they can explore. Challenge them to think of still other techniques to add to the chart. Similarly, at the creative writing center a chart can identify a selection of titles for exploration.

✔ Another application of the chart in the writing center is to list on it all the words that the students might need as they write stories. This practice makes creative writing flow more smoothly and prevents frustration for the children who really want to spell correctly but don't want to stop and ask for or look up every word in the dictionary. These charts are especially helpful for seasonal and holiday writing when interest is high and when many children may be writing on similar topics. When such charts are no longer in high demand, combine them into oversize word books to which children may continue to have access as they are interested in using them as a giant dictionary.

For several different ways in which posters and charts might be displayed, refer to Figures 29 and 30.

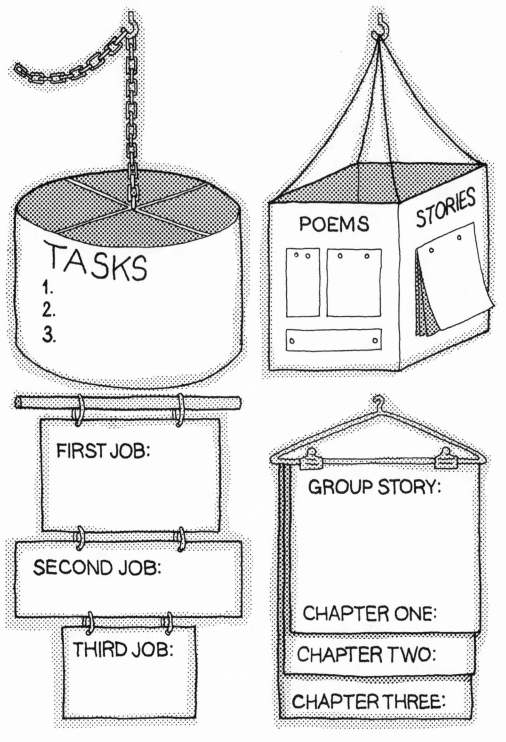

Figure 29   Chart Displays

Figure 30   Chart Displays

Preparing Activity Cards

Another feature frequently found in open classrooms is the activity card, or the task card, on which individual learning experiences are described. Some of the activities listed on the cards are presented as part of a specified sequence requiring the learner to proceed through them in a stipulated order. Other activity cards are open ended, and the pupil is free to choose any one he wants to use.

✔ If packets of task cards are kept in a box, include a face card index divider at the beginning of the set to indicate all the cards that are in that particular collection. Use a card that is of a different color than the task cards and list on it all the task cards that are included in the box. ✔ Because there may be two or more sets of activity cards relating to the same general subject, mark each set distinctively to make their identification easier. For example, use blue cards for mathematics experiences, red for reading, and yellow for art. Should task cards for different subjects be of the same color, notch the corners to help the children sort them if the cards get mixed up.

✔ Add interest to activity cards by appropriately decorating the containers in which they are kept. Containers for social studies cards might be covered, for example, with cancelled stamps or road maps. For mathematics boxes use discarded calendars. Pages from a discarded dictionary or a newspaper might do for a set of cards in language arts. Use book jackets for reading activities and sports pictures for games and fitness experiences. Sheet music is just right for brightening the music and rhythms containers, and finger-painted designs are one obvious possibility for covering boxes for art tasks.

chapter eight
Managing Daily Details in Open Classrooms

Under any circumstances teaching is a demanding job with lessons to plan, paperwork to complete, children to counsel, materials to prepare, and supplies to order. Even the most efficient professional is hard pressed to discharge promptly all her responsibilities. The problem is compounded in an open classroom, for the open teacher has materials that are much more diversified than those of a traditional teacher and her children's needs are being met on an individualized basis. However difficult these logistics may seem, there are many solutions to the challenges of arrangements and supervision during the course of the open day.

Where to Find Adult Assistance

One notable need of the open classroom is the provision of adequate supervision and resource personnel. Because so much occurs in the open setting that even the most conscientious instructor can always benefit from extra help, the participation of adult aides in schools has been increasing during the past decade. In many districts aides are hired on a yearlong contract to contribute their skills to the instructional program. Although paid aides can help things go more smoothly in the classroom, many school districts do not have funds available for this purpose and the open teacher may have to find other assistance.

The obvious solution to this enigma is the use of volunteers, who are especially appropriate in an open setting because informal learners use every source of information available. The contributions of parents, peers, and professionals are all welcome. When volunteers are sought, it is important to begin with the parents of the children themselves. ✔ At the beginning of the school year send home with the students a detailed questionnaire asking for information about parents' occupations, avocations, interests, travels, and other talents and experiences that might help children learn. Be as thorough and as specific as possible. Solicit from them names of other members of the community who might also have special skills to offer. Present several options of time commitments ranging from a single opportunity to a daily involvement (Figure 31).

Figure 31   Parent Helper Survey

Parents:

Many members of our community share their skills and information with our children in the classroom from time to time. If you could help us learn in any of these ways this year, please tell us what you would like to do and how often you would be interested in helping. Also you might suggest names of neighbors, friends, or others in the community who have special talents they too might share.

☐ Tell something interesting about the history of our area

☐ Read a story aloud to a group

☐ Do some gardening indoors or outdoors

☐ Share a special hobby

☐ Explain your job

☐ Demonstrate food preparation

☐ Show something from another country or background

☐ Bring a pet and display it

☐ Play a musical instrument

☐ Work with tools

☐ Teach an active game

☐ Teach a song

☐ Demonstrate a crafts activity

☐ Show personal films, slides, or photographs

☐ Teach a foreign language

☐ Share souvenirs of travel

☐ Build toys and play equipment

☐ Help produce a play or a puppet show

If you prefer not to help teach or make presentations, you might be able to provide an extra pair of hands when extra supervision is needed or when things need to be prepared for the children.

☐ Duplicate learning materials on the ditto machine

☐ Set up an instructional display

☐ Dictate a spelling quiz

☐ Listen to children read aloud

☐ Process new books in our media center

- [ ] Check learning aids in and out of the room
- [ ] Supervise a party
- [ ] Prepare snacks or lunches
- [ ] Sponsor a field trip experience
- [ ] Tape-record a child's original composition
- [ ] Make a bulletin board
- [ ] Collect money, notes, and other items
- [ ] Operate the audio-visual equipment
- [ ] Locate resource materials
- [ ] Work with arts and crafts
- [ ] Help with sewing and fabric experiences
- [ ] Assist with mechanical experiences
- [ ] Supervise a picnic or a play day

For each item you have checked, please indicate how often you would prefer to be considered for helping in the classroom. Also, please suggest any other possibilities of assistance that are not included on this survey.

Another source of support is available in the pool of community workers, many of whom are quite willing to explain their occupations and to demonstrate skills connected with them. ✔ The local chamber of commerce, as well as service organizations and fraternal and professional groups, should be contacted. Some towns have prepared lists of speakers who are willing to help. ✔ Military personnel often have unique backgrounds to share. ✔ Also consider the services of senior citizens. Their unpaid work can include something as simple as a regular story hour, or they can be adopted by the class as substitute grandparents-in-residence. Sometimes it is just enough to be available when a youngster wants a friend or needs to be comforted in a well-used rocking chair. Aging persons from the local area can also contribute to the pupils a sense of continuity and history as they reveal some of the changes that have occurred in the school and in the surrounding area. Many senior citizens have hobbies in the arts and crafts that should not be ignored.

A third possibility for aid is the teacher training institution. ✔ Although most preservice training programs are conducted on long-term arrangements between schools and colleges, it is appropriate to have students-in-training spend at least a few days in the open classrooms whenever time is available—for example, before and after their terms of study. Even such an occasional encounter can provide young adults with a chance to share their enthusiasm and insight with open learners. Even on a short-term basis they can assume some of the incidental chores: listening to children read, checking materials in and out of a learning center, making costumes for a play, inventing simple toys, and readying arts and crafts materials. Such occasional helpers also can assemble scrapbooks, take pictures of activities, and manufacture learning aids.

If the open teacher's relationship with another adult is to be long-range, it is essential that all parties work well together. This is especially true when procedures and expectations might be at variance; for example, an adult helper who wants to have children absolutely quiet and who demands other forms of regimentation would not be happy in an open classroom. ✔ It is wise to assess adult volunteers by asking them to serve only once in a while until it is determined that there is a mutually supportive relationship possible. After an aide is engaged to work on a fairly regular basis, the open teacher must allow the helper to participate in the decision making, for this is the only way to maintain the model of openness.

Capitalize on the strengths of aides by asking them to suggest new ways of presenting materials, preparing lessons, or supervising activities. ✔ Provide a list of jobs from which aides may select those tasks they are most interested in or best prepared to do. ✔ Set up a "Wish Book" in which there are listed special projects that need to be done when there is time. If a job is to be done in only one way, prepare written directions for the aide to follow. Allow adequate time for conferences with aides during the day, preferably at the close of school in a relaxed setting where a useful assessment of children's development can be made.

Involving Student Helpers

One other way to develop a cadet corps is by contacting teachers of older pupils in the same school district. These include junior high school or senior high school students who are interested in teaching or child care as a career or who enjoy working with children. ✔ Give special recognition to these young volunteers by providing attractive name cards labeling them as "Cadet Teachers" or "Classroom Cadre" or "Junior Teachers." Let them become deeply involved in high-interest activities such as storytelling, story reading, dramatics, working with puppets, recording original compositions on tape, playing games, and working puzzles.

✔ A related approach is to identify older children in the same school who are in need of a chance to practice their skills with younger students. This may be a simple matter of letting an older child sharpen his reading ability by reading aloud to a younger group or letting him develop self-confidence by working with subjects at a more comfortable level. There may be students who are slow in certain subject areas but are especially talented in others. In elementary schools this is often true of boys, who tend to have more learning problems than have their female counterparts. Such students could be asked to help out in subject areas in which they are competent.

Another idea is to use as coteachers children who are the same age as those children in the open classroom. Such a commitment is consistent with one of the aims of openness—the development of an awareness of individual interests and mutual needs. In the open setting children are viewed not only as learners but also as teachers. Even at the elementary level some students have more extensive knowledge and skills than the adults assigned to teach them. It is wasteful and demeaning to ignore their competencies and their natural interest in sharing what they know with their peers. Compatible children can work together as "study buddies" in a variety of situations.

✔ Students can "teach" each other if one member of a pair learns a new concept and then shares it with his friend. Permit such pairs to work together on a single assignment with one person doing the research and the other doing the writing, one completing a task and the other partner checking its accuracy, or one child pronouncing spelling words and the other taking the test.

✔ Another approach is to let each child identify his own area of expertise and then label himself as a resident expert. For example, any student who wishes to assist with spelling hard words needed for written composition can make a large cardboard placard and attach it to his work space. Such a sign might read "Dr. Wordo at your service," and the science expert might prepare a sign reading "Mr. Wizard is IN!"

✔ You might also set up a resource station manned by a changing panel of experts who take turns answering questions and giving advice. In this way no single child is tied to the responsibility for long. Decorate the consultation center with "Peanuts" or other cartoon characters, and add rugs and comfortable seats for the "clients."

✔ Still another variation on this idea is to set up a large representation of a computer manufactured from a refrigerator carton. Cut into the sides of this construction several slots identified by subject areas, and ask for pupil volunteers to sit inside this device and respond to the queries their classmates submit.

Simplifying Record Keeping

In the open classroom much of the responsibility for keeping records is transferred to the learner. This practice not only teaches the child to be accountable for his own progress, but it also frees the teacher from such routine management chores and enables her to spend her time more profitably in planning programs and conferring personally with her students. Children who are entrusted with this job from an early age are eager to assume it and are proud of their ability to do so. Record keeping is made easier for pupils when certain procedures are followed.

If it is appropriate to rotate involvements in different learning centers during the week, ask the children themselves to keep track of which areas they are to use each day. ✔ One way to facilitate this responsibility is to prepare three concentric circles of cardboard and to fasten them together with brass fasteners. On the inner circle identify the special parts of the room where materials are available for use. On the second larger circle write in the names of the children who belong to each cluster, and on the largest circle indicate some of the major activities that are to emerge from their efforts at each interest center. Each day the middle circle can be rotated to give each group a different set of learning experiences during activity periods. When groups are reassigned or when skills are changed, simply take apart the circles and attach new ones (Figure 32).

✔ Use this same general approach to assign routine classroom maintenance tasks during the day. Involve all students in the custodial care of their learning environment and apportion other responsibilities as well. Attach two concentric

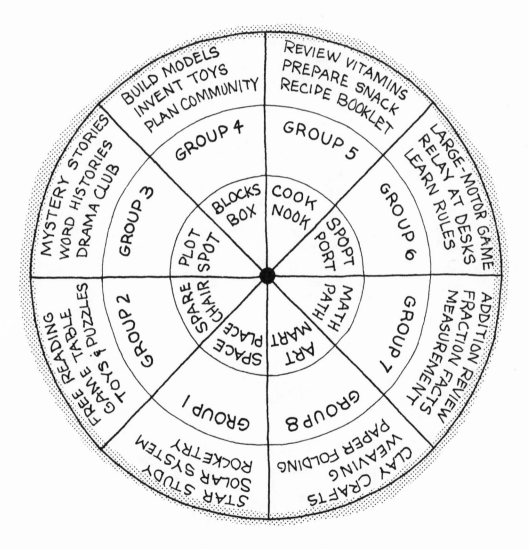

Figure 32   Task Circle

circles, an inner one with the names of the children and a larger one with their classroom jobs. Move the inner circle one space as the day begins (Figure 33).

✔ For children who have even greater freedom regarding the types of activities they may select, set up a poster on which are placed packets of ideas suggesting many different learning experiences. Give each student the privilege of choosing those items in which he is most interested (Figure 34).

✔ If it becomes useful to have children randomly choose some of their activities—for example, after they have finished their required work—set up two circles of tagboard fastened side by side on a poster and rotating freely. Individual children may spin the circles or snap the arrow spinner attached with brass fasteners (Figure 35).

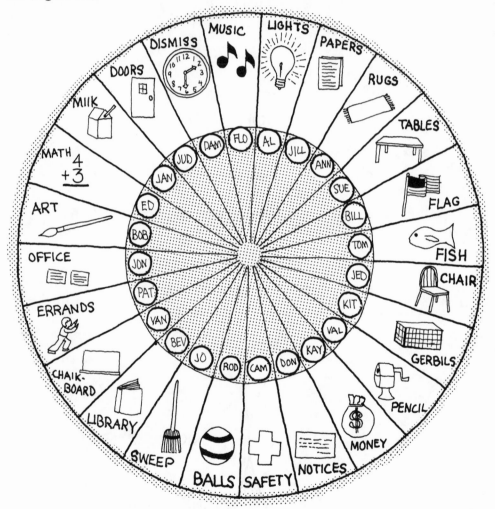

Figure 33   Duty Spinner

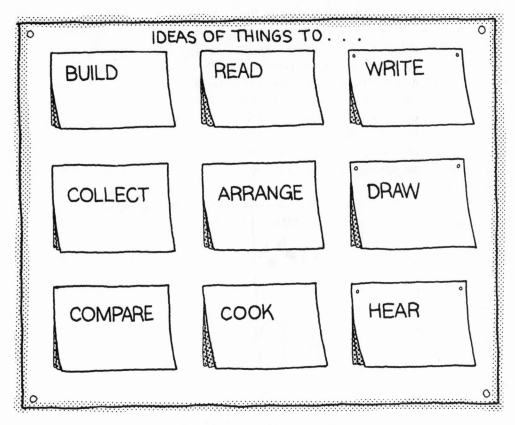

Figure 34   Activity Chart

TWIRL WHEEL OR SNAP ARROW SPINNERS

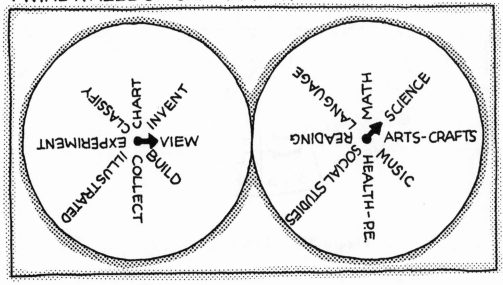

Figure 35   Twirl Wheels or Snap Arrow Spinners

Set up a self-checking attendance system to save time at the beginning of each day. ✔ Code a two-color set of name tags placed in a pocketed chart hung near the door; as the students arrive each day, have them flip over their name cards. The green side of the tag indicates that the child is present, and the red side shows he is absent. ✔ Adapt this same idea to a set of springtype clothespins clipped to a wire, each of which is labeled with a student's name; or use a set of children's self-portraits or photographs to show who is present every session. You can apply this same self-accounting approach to other records, such as the number of children eating hot lunch, the number of children riding busses, or the number of persons who have returned notices sent home by the principal (Figure 36).

✔ When children are all working at interest centers at the same time, you may need to limit the number of students at one spot. Where this limitation is important, post a large chart showing how many students are to be in that area at the same time or provide a sign-up chart to help children govern the use of the center.

✔ Since open learners are often outside the classroom in pursuit of their projects, a sign-out chalkboard placed beside the door is useful. ✔ So is a

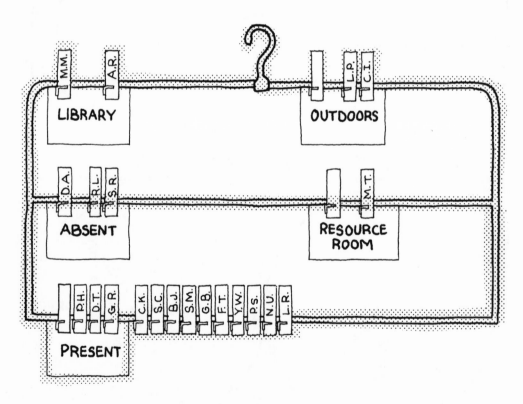

Figure 36   Attendance Checker

wooden check-out board on which a series of labeled cup hooks and miniature clocks indicates times and destinations of the children who leave the room. ✔ You can vary the sign-out procedures by gathering note paper into "prescription pads" such as are used to order medicine. When a child needs to have permission to visit another part of the building, give him such a memo to take along. ✔ When individual children need to be out of the room at times during the day, use a semicircular time clock equipped with labeled pockets into which each pupil leaving the room inserts his name and destination at the appropriate time and place (Figure 37).

If the major portion of the open day is spent in pursuit of individual learning experiences, scheduling is no problem because very few time slots need to be designated for group obligations. However, in most classrooms where open procedures are at work, there is still a responsibility for total class involvements, some of which must be arranged at the beginning of the year with special instructors in physical education, art, music, and other areas of the curriculum. There is also the need to observe all-school schedules for recess periods, lunchroom use, and dismissal times. Individual members of the class are similarly charged with remembering times to report for speech therapy, remediation in reading or mathematics, or general reinforcement in a resource room.

✔ To help the children recall this need to shift from one type of involvement to another, post prominently a chart on which the general weekly schedule is suggested (Figure 38). ✔ Or ask each child to make and decorate his own personal schedule to be taped to the side of his work space. ✔ You also can set up a series of charts that inform students of the types of activities they have selected or have been assigned during work sessions (Figure 39).

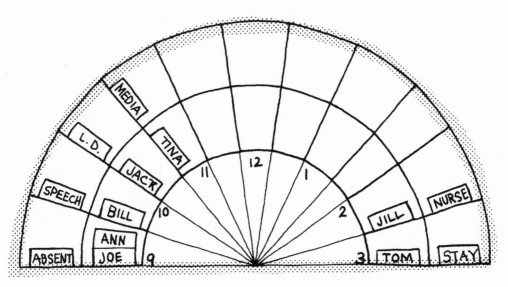

Figure 37   Attendance Chart

	MON.	TUE.	WED.	THU.	FRI.
BEFORE SCHOOL 9:00	INDEPENDENT PROJECTS				
9:30	TOTAL GROUP SESSION				
	READING INTEREST GROUPS	READING INDIV. SKILLS	READING INTEREST GROUPS	READING GROUP SKILLS	READING INDIV. PROJECTS
10:30	CONFER.	SHARE	CONFER.	CONFER.	SHARE
	INDIV. SOC. ST.	GROUP SOC. ST.	INDIV. SCIENCE	GROUP SCIENCE	INDIV. HEALTH
11:30	FITNESS BREAK				
	LUNCH and RECESS				
	FREE READING				
12:30	GROUP MATH				
	INDIV. MATH	GROUP HEALTH	INDIV. MATH	GROUP SAFETY	INDIV. MATH
1:30	GROUP LANGUAGE	IND. SPELLING	IND. WRITING	IND. SPELLING	IND. WRITING
	P.E.	GAMES	P.E.	P.E.	GAMES
2:30	IND. ARTS	GROUP MUSIC ARTS	IND. ARTS	GROUP MUSIC ARTS	IND. MUSIC

Figure 38   Modified Open Schedule in Self-Contained Room

ACTIVITY TIME PLANNING POSTER

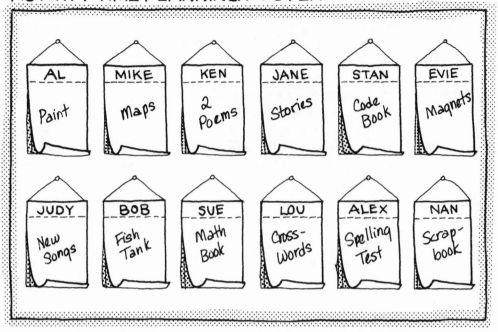

CONTRACT CHART

LEARNING CENTER RECORD

	WHERE DID YOU WORK?				
	M	T	W	T	F
Andy	6	6	6	4	7
Susan	3	5	1	6	7
Karen	5	2	2	3	7
Dan	1	3	5	1	7
meg	6	A.B.	6	2	7
Walt	4	3	4	3	7
chuck	1	5	2	3	7

Figure 39   Activity Charts

✔ Another way to self-schedule learning is to set up a large poster pin map on which the activity centers are specified. Each child is responsible for placing his pin, number coded to his name, in the spot on the map indicating where he will be studying during the independent learning period (Figure 40).

✔ Enliven the self-checking of student assignments by investing a small amount of money in commercial stampers. Use a date stamper to indicate when each project is completed, and use a variety of cartoon stampers to help children express their satisfaction with their work.

✔ Show the pupils how to set up graphs for recording their activities and their achievements. One simple device is a grid on which children's names are listed on one axis and skills or activities are written on the other axis. Each student

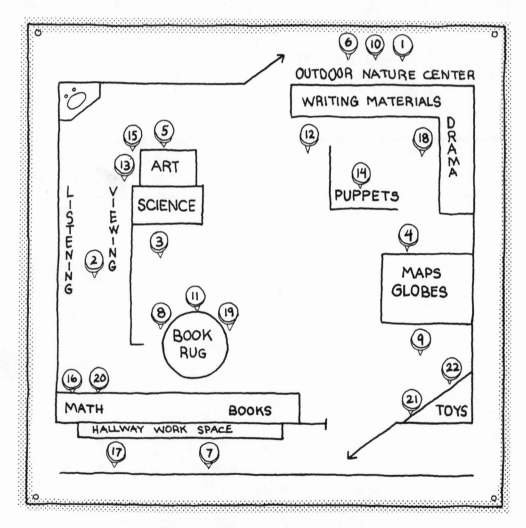

Figure 40   Projects Pin Map

places his initials in the appropriate square when he has completed each activity or skill on the chart. ✔ Another version of the graph involves each child in registering with a bar or a line his own progress in subject areas such as mathematics or spelling; this graph visually reinforces his accomplishments and his improvement in the several areas of the curriculum. A color coded graph furthers this notion as the child colors in with crayons or colored pencils the areas in which he has been working. Simply by glancing at these colors it is possible to determine if a given student needs to be redirected to some other area of study.

✔ To further long-range education planning among the class members, give each student a plan book like those that are customarily issued to teachers at the beginning of the school year. Each week designate a brief period for the pupils to fill in the pages of the plan book with appropriate activities they would like to undertake, and then later let them check off each project as it is completed.

✔ Salvage manila folders that are discarded from offices. Open some of these up and cut them in half in such a way that half-size pieces can be stapled to full-size folders to make a pocketed holder. Give these to the students for storing papers and for containing their records of progress in skills development.

✔ When materials are checked out of the room for home use, keep a record of them by making a chart on which each child has his own library card pocket with his name printed on it. Attach a library card to each book and to each major piece of equipment that may be borrowed for home use. When a child takes such an item home, he simply removes the library card from the equipment being borrowed and places the card in the pocket with his name on it.

Controlling Noise

The open classroom is likely to be somewhat noisier than the traditional classroom. During much of the day there is general movement of children as individual students find materials and groups suitable to their own personal goals. Although the open teacher is not terribly sensitive to constructive noise and confusion, there are some situations in which noise does become bothersome to the children in the room. Some open classrooms are located in old schools where walls and floors reflect sound and where ceilings are high. If the level of noise is distracting the children or bothering other teachers and the school principal, it is helpful to consider several techniques that might ameliorate the situation.

✔ One approach to the problem of acoustics is to fix on the walls carpet squares salvaged from furniture stores or purchased at rug dealers. You can use similar items for seating during informal activities and can stack them out of the way when the floor space is needed for other experiences.

✔ Pastel styrofoam egg cartons that are laced together with colorful lengths of yarn can be put on walls to cut noise. Styrofoam meat trays are useful in this manner. ✔ Long panels of unbleached muslin or fabric acquired at a remnant sale are also appropriate, particularly if children are able to decorate them with original block printing or other media.

✔ Dampen the reflection of sound from ceiling surfaces by suspending a surplus parachute or chutelike panels from the light fixtures or from the ceiling itself. ✔ A similar idea is to distribute randomly about the classroom large sections of pressed-fiber acoustical tile on which designs have been added without impairing the sound absorbency of the material.

✔ If children are using tools and equipment on table surfaces, cover the tables with salvaged panels of beaverboard or other pressed fiberboard. Use this same material for isolation booths erected on the tops of desks or tables. ✔ In the reading center use cushions, pillows, and beanbags made from remnant pieces of cloth and assembled by the parents of the children.

✔ Depend on visual or auditory signals to tell the children when the noise rises beyond a tolerable level. Flick the lights, play a soft chord on a piano or a set of tone bells, or use a combination of green, yellow, and red lights to cue the class. ✔ Continue to be aware of the ebb and flow of activities, and when certain involvements produce too much noise, change the pace by shifting children's interests to storytelling, quiet music, a sit-down circle game, or an auditory discrimination skill.

✔ Select carefully the types of materials used in the room. Cardboard boxes and soft plastic containers are much less noisy than metal ones. Shoes are more of a problem than slippers or stockings. Blocks and other construction elements made of styrofoam or cardboard present fewer difficulties than wooden ones.

Handling Problems of Storage

An efficient method of storing materials in the open classroom is indispensable for three important reasons. First, there is generally such a wide variety of devices, equipment, and materials in the open classroom that good organization is the only way to reduce clutter and confusion. Second, because most of the learning in an open classroom is self-selected, instructional items must be readily accessible to the children to preserve their spontaneity and enthusiasm. Finally, a good management scheme in the classroom enables the children to practice their responsibility for returning each item to its proper place after they are done with it. A simple and attractive method of storage not only facilitates the matching of contents with containers but also makes it fun for the students to assume this task. When considering places and spaces, think of the unconventional as well as the expected.

✔ Salvage picnic baskets, market baskets, and other food containers to hold books. This idea is especially appropriate for learning materials that relate to nutrition and the preparation of foods. Other theme related containers might include an old suitcase to hold maps and realia dealing with foreign countries, a recipe box for food task cards, a woman's purse for play money and change-counting activity cards, a small tool box for occupational activities, a sewing kit for experiences connected with fabrics or weaving, a record holder to store music experience items, or a large stationery box as a place for materials used in letter writing and story writing.

✔ You can use mobile carts to hold social studies material concerning transportation if the carts are decorated to look like locomotives, fire engines, racers, and airplanes. Even a child's coaster wagon can be adapted for storage by adding colorful elements made from cardboard cartons.

✔ Use pieces of clothing that are appropriate for specific learning tasks. A carpenter's apron can hold paper, pencils, and measuring implements; a pair of denim shorts is useful for storing small notebooks, pens, and pencils; clothespin bags, shoebags, and other pocketed items are useful for storing tape cassettes, small boxed games, and other items. Let the children take turns wearing the storage garment and taking the responsibility for its contents.

✔ Suspend a clear plastic umbrella from the ceiling and use it as a storage spot for soft items such as hats for dressup, and pillows and cushions for on-the-floor studying. Add a series of spring-type clothespins on colorful lengths of yarn for temporary hangers.

✔ To store individual students' goods, particularly when the class members no longer have their own desk space, provide a labeled location for coats and other apparel by attaching hooks at random places throughout the classroom. ✔ Also, give each student a tote tray for pencils, crayons, paper, and other personal possessions; a set of plastic dishpans, each one labeled with the owner's name is one handy example. ✔ You can cut down a set of large plastic jugs, each one labeled with colorful fabric or plastic tape, but remember to leave the handle intact for ease of carrying. ✔ A set of three-gallon ice cream cartons can be arranged to hold a great variety of materials, especially if the cartons are stapled or tied together and stacked horizontally between two sturdy book cases or comparable supports.

✔ Set up groups of shoeboxes for storage, cutting away one end of each box. Use these for science materials, for individual students' goods, or for sets of activity cards on different subjects.

✔ An easy way to carry materials around the room is to convert compartmented soft drink carriers into tote trays for cans, jars of paint, sets of activity cards, or collections of books.

✔ Store large irregularly shaped items in colorfully decorated self-standing shopping bags with handles. ✔ Or suspend on pegboard hooks net bags such as are used to market potatoes or citrus fruits.

✔ Where there is a need for storing large pictures, paintings, or pieces of oversize cardboard, invert an ordinary chair and use its legs as a holder. ✔ To store bulky books, records, large activity cards, posters, and other comparable items, salvage a dish drainer or a record holder.

✔ Collect matching transparent plastic boxes such as those sold in hobby shops or in sewing centers. Arrange them in vertical stacks to conserve shelf space and to permit children to view the contents of each box.

✔ Wax coated half-gallon or gallon cardboard milk cartons can be stapled together to make a set of mailboxes for distributing papers or for storing finished art projects. Cut away only a portion of the open end to insure greater rigidity. Another type of mailbox is easily constructed by tying together sets of tubes that are found inside gift wrapping.

✔ Gather sets of books in an original "book house" complete with a carrying handle. To make this item, find a large cardboard box and cut down the sides so that books can be placed inside. Shape the top flaps to form the peak of a roof, but leave holes in them for a handle. Decorate this book house according to the type of books you have. Mystery stories deserve a haunted house, and stories about cars should be stored in a garage. Animal stories would logically belong in a zoo.

✔ Pocketed oaktag folders are easily adapted for storage because they can be purchased in colors and coded to different subject areas or to levels of difficulty of tasks. Fill these pocketed folders with individual envelopes containing activity cards, or give each child his own folder, each with a variety of task cards stored on one side and the finished papers and other projects stored in the other.

✔ Rescue discarded manila mailing envelopes that are often found in school offices. Accumulate them in sets that match in size and shape. If it is possible, use only those envelopes that still have flaps that open and close. Cut a cardboard box to the size of these mailers and write the contents of each envelope on each flap. The children can quickly flip through the flaps to locate the task cards or learning materials they need.

✔ Convert the drawers in the larger pieces of office furniture into accessible labeled containers for children to use. For example, shallow drawers in the teacher's desk are good files for worksheets and puzzle pages, and deeper drawers can hold large pieces of instructional equipment. See to it that these drawers are easily removable so that they can be moved when they are needed in different parts of the classroom. Have the drawers in file cabinets equally available for student materials, with each section of the larger compartments adequately labeled to serve students' needs.

Consider the storage possibilities of commonplace materials readily available to most teachers. Juice cans, ice cream cartons, and cardboard compartments are useful for storage. ✔ Recycled shallow hosiery boxes can house many materials: they are convenient compartments for puzzles, for worksheets, or for activity cards. They are also handy for self-contained sets of pictures which prompt creative composition. Whenever such shallow boxes are used, however, remember to cut a notch near one end of the lid and staple the lid to the box so the lid will not get lost. Where suitable, staple to the lid directions for using the items stored inside the box, and also include the information needed for the child to check the accuracy of his work (Figures 41 and 42).

✔ Convert a shallow closet or set of shelves into a storage center containing only those materials relating to a single theme or area of study. Place one child in charge of its general maintenance (Figure 43).

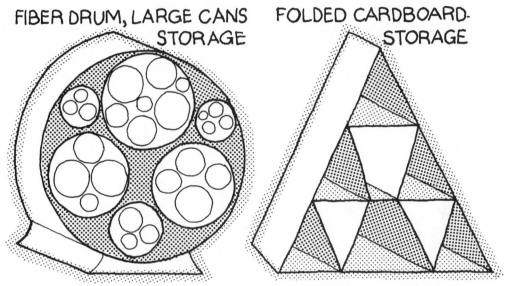

Figure 41   Storage Possibilities

Figure 42   Ice Cream Carton Storage

Inside the cabinet (labels): TAPES, PICTURE FILE, FILM STRIPS, RECORD PLAYER

On the door:

BOOKS READ
TITLE ★★★
TITLE ★
TITLE ★★★★
TITLE ★★
TITLE

CHECK BOOKS OUT.....

Figure 43   Resource Closet

✔ Carve a large cardboard box on the diagonal, and cut slots into the sides to hold other sturdy pieces of cardboard that serve as dividers. Use this oversize compartment to hold large items such as sheets of paper, posterboard, or completed art projects. A set of smaller boxes that fit vertically inside these dividers placed on the diagonal cut can serve as self-contained storage elements.

✔ Space along a long dowel rod the spring-type "bulldog" clips and place the rod across an opening cut out of the top of a large cardboard box. Such clips singly or in pairs can hold charts, examples of student work, and posters.

✔ Boxes with hinged lids are especially appropriate for holding a variety of learning materials. The lid of a cigar box makes a compact flannelboard, for example, and the flannel figures can be stored inside the box itself. You can also use the lid of a flat thin box; notched and stapled to the box, the lid makes a handy lap board for writing. Salvage or make from scrap material large hinged wooden boxes that can serve both as seating during the day and as storage units when school is over.

Order from Disorder: Clean-Up Time

Because children in the open classroom spend so much of their time in individual tasks, and because they use such a variety of learning aids and devices, it is not surprising to discover a measure of clutter during the course of an open classroom's day. This disarray sometimes works against the open teacher because the casual passerby is inclined to view it as hindering good learning. Such a conventional viewpoint ignores the fact that most of the order and structure in the children's lives is arranged by adults and is not chosen by the children themselves. When children are left to pursue their own interests, their organization of time and materials generally reflects the impulses of the moment.

Of course, in a limited area where twenty-five or thirty children are interacting there is some need to have reasonable order. Children can understand the necessity to return the classroom to its original condition at the end of each instructional day if they recognize the rights of children other than themselves. As the open teacher reinforces the notion that consideration for others is the measure of a well-ordered life, the children see that the same self-discipline that guides self-directed learning also prompts them to keep the classroom shipshape.

✔ To implement an active involvement in clean-up activities, you might include these obligations as a part of each child's written contract so that each pupil knows he is not only to use the learning materials and the area in which they are found, but is also to restore them to their original place and condition. A checklist included in each contract will serve as a convenient reminder.

✔ To make it easier for children to care for the classroom, display large posters that remind them in humorous fashion; pictures of animals and enlarged cartoon characters can stimulate good housekeeping habits. Use these posters in conjunction with checklists that are posted in each interest center.

✔ You can minimize the possibility of conflict with other adults in the school by involving them directly in the program. For example, the school custodian who is encouraged to volunteer a few minutes of his time explaining the use of his tools, his cleaning duties, and his commitment to keeping the entire school attractive and efficient is less likely to complain about a messy classroom and is more apt to have the children's cooperation in keeping it well ordered. Similarly, the school principal who is asked to help children convert cardboard cartons into learning centers is not as inclined to view such items as an assortment of junk.

✔ Encourage children to assume their clean-up responsibilities by showing them a willingness to participate in the communal chores. Because all persons working and living in an area are helping to disarrange it, refrain from talking about "your mess;" instead, refer to clutter as "our mess." The teacher who picks up and puts away items that she did not personally dislocate sets a strong silent example for her pupils.

✔ Allow individual children to volunteer overall responsibility for areas in which they have a special interest. Let such assistants issue monitory "tickets" to those students who forget their obligations for neatness.

✔ When special help is needed for one-time-only jobs, you can set up a large "Help Wanted!" sign. Describe the task in the style of a classified newspaper advertisement, stipulating the special abilities required for its completion.

✔ Have on hand sets of child-sized cleaning implements and provide a convenient storage place for them. Hooks and hangers holding brooms and mops in plain view make it easy for pupils to help.

✔ To challenge children to complete their jobs, particularly when time is short, set an ordinary kitchen timer for a specified number of minutes and see if the students can "beat the clock" as they work. This technique gives the class a definite number of minutes for the job and a set stopping time. ✔ Another variation of this approach is to set the timer and hide it somewhere in the classroom. When the timer rings, ask any pupil not working or not finished with his job to perform a brief silly stunt to give the group an informal break.

✔ Help the children to be more aware of the impact of the classroom's appearance by asking the custodian each day to evaluate the condition of the classroom and to leave a "grade" on the chalkboard. Keep a chart or other record of the children's success in this joint endeavor.

✔ Label clusters of desks or tables with real names of streets and roads in the students' home community. Make simple signposts to hold these labels. Organize the work crew into a "block party" and have a low-key competition between groups.

✔ Interest in clean-up time can be increased by painting a box for debris in a manner resembling a garbage truck. Place this receptacle on a coaster wagon or on a set of casters for greater mobility. ✔ Cover a large waste basket with travel posters or with posters exhorting children not to litter. ✔ On each trash can make a conical hat after the fashion of the Paris kiosks. ✔ Convert an ordinary waste box into a "trash monster" for the students to feed.

✔ Designate different custodial jobs in the room by referring to a rotating list of children who have shown a willingness to help with them. One simple method is to use spring-type clothespins, each labeled with either a job or a name. For a more random selection of helpers, use as spinners a series of pointing fingers on a hand cut from stiff cardboard. ✔ You can add prestige to each job by giving it the title of a community occupation such as "Maintenance Man," "Environmental Engineer," "Repair Service," or "Chief Custodian." Distribute arm bands and badges that identify each role.

Aids for the General Routine

✔ When specified times of day are set aside for special classes such as physical education, music, and art, help the children remember these obligations by posting in the classroom a series of symbols associated with each special activity and by placing a replica of a clock face alongside each symbol. Set each clock to its appropriate time. ✔ For a central point where all schedules are posted for the week, place in the center of the room a round fiber drum salvaged from a commercial bakery or laundry and painted a bright color. Use this kiosk to post schedules and other important announcements.

✔ Scheduling the teacher's time is just as important as scheduling children's time. Reduce the impatience of students who need assistance with individual projects by asking each pupil to make a colorful "HELP!" flag that can be placed on a desk where there is need. Occasionally scan the room to see whose flag is raised.

✔ To facilitate movement about the classroom when there is need to help the children individually, equip the teacher's chair with casters, or better yet, acquire a swivel chair on casters.

✔ When the children need to move from highly individualized learning into a more structured group setting, provide an informal activity to serve as a bridge between the two types of involvement. This helps the students to change gears and it gives them time to put away their materials and prepare for the group experience. Music serves this purpose nicely; use some of the songs the children have learned as cues to indicate the end of one type of learning and the beginning of another.

✔ Be sure to label all audio-visual equipment and other mechanical items with instructions and diagrams to help the children learn how to use them properly. ✔ Label in outline fashion all the tools that are to be hung up on a pegboard panel or stored on shelves. ✔ Mark all storage receptacles with sample items or pictures of their contents. This will save you instruction and filing time.

✔ Use color coding to facilitate the location of materials. For example, color the tips of book spines with squares of fabric tape to show which books are easy and which ones are more challenging. Sort materials by subject area or by topic in different colored boxes. Color code supplementary items with basal materials or a matching workbook and textbook.

✔ You can add interest to daily helper chores by making simple costumes appropriate for each responsibility—a carpenter's smock or a kitchen apron is useful for many tasks. Use tote trays, a small suitcase, an oversize purse, or a briefcase to store the implements used in different classroom jobs.

chapter nine
Encouraging
Self-Discipline

Building Appropriate Behaviors

Discipline in the open setting prompts the teacher to develop personal expectations of children that are consistent with their natural inclinations and with their need to help direct their own conduct. The open teacher responds to children as she would to any people who have deep sensitivities and a desire for acceptance by their peers and by the adults with whom they associate. Simply by being aware of the characteristics of children, she makes it easy for them to behave well. For example, she knows that children must move about during the day, so she does not make students restless by requiring them to stay for long periods in one place. She also realizes that a child who is thirsty or in need of a bathroom is not likely to concentrate on his tasks. She responds to children's desire to share experiences by allowing children to work together on common projects. She no longer dispenses individual privileges to her students, nor does she develop long lists of rules.

The open classroom should serve as a miniature model of a democratic society. Because a sense of civic responsibility begins at the very earliest ages, the open teacher involves her pupils in setting reasonable guidelines for their actions in the classroom. Children who understand the necessity of such rules and who help to generate them during the school year are likely to consider them reasonable and just expectations. Each person is charged with the job of monitoring his own behavior. The teacher distinguishes between discipline imposed and discipline assumed, and she knows that the true measure of a self-disciplined class is how well students behave when she is not present in the room.

The open teacher stresses the element of trust. Just as she believes each child can decide what to learn and how to learn, she is also confident he can help decide what his behavior should be. She allows for errors in social judgments, and she accepts mistakes in social interactions in the same way that she accepts errors in cognitive learning. Even when children deliberately misbehave, she still maintains an underlying attitude of trust. She differentiates between motives and actions, and she accepts best intentions even if the outcomes are not acceptable. She does not hesitate to remind children when they have failed to act acceptably, but she uses indirect methods rather than commands. "I think you have forgotten how loud to talk in the room," or "Do you know why we need to wait turns at the pencil sharpener?" or "Is it reasonable to expect people to be able to study with all this shuffling about?" conveys the message much more effectively than "Stop talking!" or "Don't push!" or "Sit down!"

Another task of the open teacher is to make it easy for the children to be good. The open teacher does this by complimenting and praising rather than nagging and criticizing. The teacher closely observes her children and compliments them when they are responding well. Her positive comments serve as reinforcement for more good conduct. Further, she sees that the surroundings are conducive to enthusiastic learning and proper deportment. The room is attractive and pleasant. The ventilation and lighting are well regulated. There are ample materials to use. The teacher treats her students in such a way that there is no sense of competition for her attention and favors. Children take pride in being able to dismiss themselves from class at the end of the day and to enter the building when they arrive in the morning, instead of waiting dutifully in line for admission or dismissal. They cherish the right to leave the room and work in the hallway, in the media center, and in some other distant part of the building without direct adult supervision.

Finally, the open teacher respects children as human beings. Just as she expects them to show consideration and good manners toward each other and toward her, so she displays toward them the same measure of courtesy that she wants them to reciprocate. She does not interrupt their conversations unless an interjection is absolutely necessary. She practices with her students the simple social amenities such as "Please," "Thank you," and "I'm sorry." She listens to children just as intently as she wants them to respond to her. She laughs as they laugh and she suffers with them when they weep. She is a friend to those who want her friendship and she is cordial to all the rest.

Suggestions for Managing Deportment

In addition to being a special person, the open teacher needs to have at hand a repertoire of management techniques that she can use to help build appropriate behaviors in the classroom. The following list of "bright ideas" is a practical source of assistance.

✔ From the first contact, you should begin to know each child well. Learn each name promptly and pronounce it accurately. See if there is anything special about each child's name, a literal meaning, for instance, or an indication of a national origin. ✔ Ask each pupil to make an unusual name tag to wear as a label during the first few days of school and to use as a desk marker later on. Suggest that each child's tag reflect something personal—a hobby, a summer experience, or a rebus representation of the name or its meaning.

✔ It is a good idea to exchange personal communications with children during the year. Before the term begins make a chart of students' birthdays. Purchase a set of birthday cards and prepare them for distribution by marking the mailing date under the corner of the envelope where the stamp will be placed. ✔ Write children letters even before the opening of school, exchanging such items of mutual interest as the name of pets, hobbies, favorite activities, pictures, travels, and summer experiences. During the year make it a habit to pass along through written notes compliments about the pupils. Be ready as well to use the telephone for sharing good news.

✔ Ask the children the first day of class to find examples of community rules, especially those that can be represented with pictures. Use pictures and symbols of these rules to construct charts as reminders of the generalizations for good behavior that the children agree upon. Replicas of traffic signs are especially appropriate to this activity, for they can be worked into slogans such as "STOP . . . to think about others," or "NO PARKING . . . on the teacher's desk!"

✔ A "Time Out" booth made from a large cardboard carton is convenient for children who need to be away from the rest of the class for brief periods. Let the students decorate this compartment in a cheerful fashion and designate it either as a "Hot Spot" for children who need to regain self-control, or as an "Office" for pupils who need a special measure of privacy.

✔ Posters made of amusing baby pictures or photographs of the children themselves can help remind the class of the suggestions for good room behavior. Humorous pictures of animals also draw students' attention to these important generalizations.

✔ Behavior problems often are remedied when a teacher assigns persons who have special problems to be in charge of areas in which they have difficulty. For example, the child who has trouble keeping his own area clean could be asked to serve briefly as the "chief sanitation engineer." The child who has trouble getting to school regularly or on time might be placed in charge of general attendance procedures.

✔ Offer the children at the outset of the year a contract in which are listed guarantees of what they may reasonably expect of you during the term. You could call the contract a "Bill of Rights" and print the following on a simulated parchment document:

1. You have the right to fair treatment.

2. You may learn as fast as you want to.

3. You may help choose what you want to know.

4. You are entitled to a friendly teacher.

Ask each child to assess his own strengths and weaknesses and to develop a similar contract detailing his own goals and plans during the year.

✔ When an individual child has a special behavior problem, help him define the difficult situation—the stimulus for his misbehavior—reducing it to simple, manageable elements. Then help the child chart the number of times the stimulus arises and how often he is able effectively to cope with it.

✔ Although the most effective long-range reinforcement is social approval, some children need frequent tangible rewards to help them behave better. If this is the case, instead of giving students pieces of candy or money, make and use coupon books of privileges that are of interest to the children involved. Issue the same coupon booklet to each child at the beginning of the week or the month. Whenever there is a need for a tangible reminder, remove one of the coupons from the book. ✔ You could reverse this procedure and issue to children coupons that can be accumulated in booklet form, one coupon for each appropriate behavior. At the end of a designated period of time, allow all the pupils to "spend" those privileges that they possess.

✔ Use humorous names for people who forget some of the principles of good conduct, placing a series of funny posters about the room as reminders. For example, a "Shouter Outer" is a good label for the person who finds it difficult to wait his turn for recognition in a group; this fault may be illustrated with a comical picture of a hippopotamus with its mouth open. The "Grubby Grabber" might be suggested by a cartoon of an octopus whose difficulty is the inability to keep his hands off other people's possessions.

✔ When positive reinforcement is necessary, designate a certain day on which any child who is complimented for a special accomplishment must, in turn, commend someone else in the room. ✔ Also, send the "Happygram," a simple duplicated yellow form that resembles a telegram. Decorate this with a smiling face, write favorable comments, and send it home.

✔ Puppets can dramatize appropriate deportment, particularly when children forget how to behave. Puppets are also especially effective in settling the inevitable disputes that arise. Let the children, through the puppets, act out the situations, and encourage each participant to suggest ways in which the situation might be handled. When two children disagree on a point, give each of them a puppet, seat them face to face on two chairs, and ask them to act out a solution to their disagreement.

✔ Help children to remember important generalizations by giving them interesting objects as reminders. A smooth stone to feel in a pocket or an inexpensive ring can be useful. ✔ A small sign placed in a humorously decorated holder at the child's work space and a pop-up card inside his desk are also handy reminders. ✔ Another idea is to purchase an easy, inexpensive framed puzzle. Tell the child that he may have one piece every hour he passes without forgetting the behavior in question. Also mention that every time he does misbehave he must forfeit one piece. Challenge him to see how quickly he can accumulate and put together all the pieces. Let him borrow the puzzle for home practice when he is done.

✔ Involve the children in communal efforts toward good behavior by sponsoring a school-wide courtesy week. Engage the class in making posters, inventing slogans, scheduling films, and creating skits to share with other rooms. Make an effort to match children with their problems: the child who has difficulty remembering not to interrupt might be encouraged to develop a poster reminding other students of this type of inconsideration.

✔ Illustrate a personal sense of human fallibility and keep the children on their toes by making an occasional ridiculous mistake. This can be something as simple as an absurd error in mathematics computation, a quaintly original spelling of a word, or just an upside-down notice posted on the bulletin board. Promote a contest in which the class tries to catch these "Weirdities," and present some nonsensical award to the winner.

✔ Permit the class members to express dissatisfaction with themselves and circumstances in the room by establishing a "Bug Box" prominently located for anonymous notes of criticism and suggestion. Submitted items can become the basis for problem-solving discussions with the class.

✔ At the beginning of the school year develop the analogy of the classroom as a spaceship in which students will all be housed for a trip of nine or ten months that will take them to a distant planet with a name such as "Sixto" or "Crypterion." Enlist their help in decorating the room with portholes. Post a chart of some of the other celestial bodies through which they will pass en route; "Lingua" and "Musica" are two examples. Make a miniature rocket from a refrigerator carton. Suspend aluminum foil stars from the ceiling. Point out that such a trip may cause special problems, and encourage the children to suggest ways in which their behavior might reveal consideration of their fellow passengers.

✔ Whenever there is a disagreement between two students, ask each one to tell the dispute from the viewpoint of the other person only. Have immediately available two pairs of slip-on shoes large enough for any child in the room. Have each disputant put on the other person's shoes while he is telling the opposite side of the story.

Motivating Good Conduct Through Enjoyment

The open teacher is also aware of techniques that help to build an esprit de corps, a pride children feel in being a member of her class. In a room where fun is a daily occurrence and where pleasure is just as important as hard work, children are likely to want to cooperate with the teacher and to consider the needs of their classmates. Many of the ideas that help in this regard are just everyday touches that many teachers overlook. The unexpected events and the unusual approaches such as those that follow help make children happy and help make happy children better behaved.

✔ Build a "Joke in the Box" for children to fill with riddles, jokes, and cartoons. Design the box in such a way that it pops open to reveal its contents. Use this item to break the daily routine or to serve as a special notice for work well done.

✔ Designate an occasional "Project Day" on which children are allowed to bring to school any project or hobby that they wish to work on during the day. Arrange a general sharing time for these special activities, and see how each one can be made relevant to the regular curriculum.

✔ Provide special places in the room for collections of objects that are assembled by the pupils. These might include a specific hobby, such as a collection of stamps, buttons, or dolls; or a communal gathering of objects of beauty, such as feathers, stones, leaves, or magazine pictures. For adequate display of such items set aside a special part of the bulletin board. For another display area, line boxes with scraps of satin or velvet to make an "Art Park" hanging display.

✔ Designate a portion of the bulletin board as a "Graffiti Spot" where children may write their own personal thoughts and messages, or may post items of special interest. A variation of this idea is to cover a large table with craft paper and allow pupils to doodle on the surface.

✔ When you are marking papers, let each child indicate special words for work well done: "Groovy" or "Super-Duper" might be chosen. On special occasions cut out colorful comic figures and attach them to papers that warrant recognition.

✔ You can make use of a variety of room furnishings and decorations. Collect chairs of several sizes and colors. Explore secondhand furniture stores for pieces to salvage. ✔ Hang plants in every window in the classroom. ✔ Suspend small prisms, mirrors, and pieces of colored glass or foil in the direct sunlight entering through windows. ✔ Use yellow balloons marked with smiling faces to brighten dark corners. ✔ Make an entryway into the room that requires the children to climb through a hole cut in the side of a large cardboard box.

✔ When it is useful to cluster children, find unusual ways to identify groups. Use the first letter of students' last names, or group students by color of hair, birthday months, or types of clothing. You might want to label groups with names from the animal world: pride, gaggle, covey, clutch. Think of interesting names from cartoons or other sources: The Garwood Gang, the Brady Bunch, the Morehouse Mob. Make appropriate labels to identify each set of children.

✔ Reward outstanding achievement with extra trading stamps or discount coupons solicited from the parents of the children. Issue these tokens as classroom scrip to purchase small treats or privileges. When enough tokens have been earned, convert them at a redemption center for a book, a game, or some other object that might be enjoyed by all members of the class. ✔ Set aside certain days as "Prize Days" when every child gets special notice for the achievement of which he is most proud. ✔ Set up a "Hall of Fame" to which children name new candidates each week.

✔ Keep absentees in close touch with the classroom happenings by collecting special materials during long-term separations from the group. These might include all the items distributed to the class as a whole, letters, notes, pictures, and greeting cards made by students. ✔ If children are hospitalized or otherwise confined, encourage class members to collect jokes, riddles, puzzles, comic books, and other interesting items for their absent classmate. Make arrangements for personal telephone calls by close friends during the school day.

✔ You can develop a strong classroom identification by letting the children make pennants and banners which only the class can keep. Stimulate the group to select official class colors; make up a brief slogan. Attach each banner to a stick and apportion the banners among students who will carry them to all-school assemblies and play days. Use such banners on poles as rallying points during field trips and other off-campus excursions.

✔ During the late winter doldrums set aside certain days for unexpected celebrations: "Backwards Day," "Thomas Edison's Birthday," "Art Day," and "Book Day" are a few examples.

✔ Maintain a communal scrapbook containing outstanding samples of student work. Have this on display for examination by parents and other visitors. Make a point to see that each child is amply represented with original stories, pictures, and other products. ✔ Exchange pupil projects with teachers in other classrooms. ✔ Set up a carnival arrangement in the hallway or the lobby with student work on display.

✔ Decorate the room by placing in strong sunlight plastic bags filled with water tinted with food coloring. Use these same containers for goldfish by suspending them in shaded areas to protect the fish.

✔ You can set aside a cardboard box into which a child may crawl when he wants to get cozy in an out-of-the-way place. Pad the box with several cushions. Allow the students to draw or paint pictures on the surface of this box. Or use one of the surfaces as a "Love Wall" on which children may post poems, greetings, pictures, and other happy thoughts.

✔ Much can be done when it rains. Keep a special collection of games, puzzles, and other activities to be used only during rainy days. Store such items in a colorful opened umbrella suspended from the ceiling. ✔ Help the students to find examples of beauty on rainy days; give a prize for the first person to notice a rainbow; take a walk in the rain; look at the world through yellow cellophane.

✔ Wherever children are required to wait for service—in a cafeteria or in a bus line—place some small booklets in a box for them to use. Include collections of jokes, cartoons, mental arithmetic problems, riddles, tongue twisters, paperback books, or daily newspapers.

✔ Salvage a mannikin from a department store or a dress shop. After you have decorated it in a clever costume, use it as a holder for important reminders or as a delivery service for personal notes to students. ✔ A classroom mascot made by stuffing with old rags a set of men's clothing also is fun to pin notes onto.

✔ Rescue from the school office pieces of purple carbon paper left over from making duplicator masters. Let the students use these carbons to trace their own work, then run them off on the duplicator using the one good side of discarded paper.

✔ Wear an unusual vest or smock and use the pockets for cards on which there are posed interesting questions, problems to solve, puzzles, and other challenges to children's thinking. You might also pin other slips of paper to the garment, occasionally rip one slip off, and read for the children something special written on it: "You have five minutes to draw the silliest picture you can think of," or "For the next ten minutes talk to anybody in the room about anything you care to discuss." ✔ Another idea is to make a simple garment of fabric on which children have drawn colorful pictures or designs with permanent felt-tip markers.

✔ Declare a "Topsy Turvy Day" to stimulate enthusiasm. Sing holiday songs out of season. Reverse the general schedule of the day. Wear items of clothing backwards. Try to read simple stories from right to left. Communicate in secret code. Wear garments that do not match each other.

✔ You can enhance patriotic sensitivity by issuing to each child a miniature flag and a spool to serve as its standard. When the Pledge of Allegiance or other civic rituals are performed, show the children how to perform a hand salute. Parade the flag around the classroom. Students will enjoy the patriotism and the feeling of belonging to a group.

✔ Learn a few magic tricks to perform when interest is waning or when children need to wait. Teach these feats to students. ✔ Make a collection of magic items for the students to fondle when they are feeling anxious or upset; a magic ring, a magic coin, a rabbit's foot, a buckeye, a smooth stone, or a miniature horseshoe are several possibilities.

✔ Let the classroom windows be a medium through which the class can communicate with the world. Decorate individual panes seasonally. ✔ Purchase or salvage some cheerful curtains. ✔ Post children's art work prominently for passersby to see. ✔ Write on the windows such personal greetings as "Happy Birthday, Susie Brown."

✔ Flowers in season will decorate the area. Try to locate a small plot for a garden near the classroom or make a small indoor hothouse by sectioning off a sunny window sill with sheets of clear plastic. Have available a variety of interesting vases to display the flowers that children bring to share.

✔ The pointer used by children to indicate items on the chalkboard can be made safer by stuffing an ordinary garden glove and inserting the pointer into the index finger of the glove. Then tape the cuff of the glove to the shaft of the pointer.   ✔ A giant replica of a magnifying glass and a pair of spectacles also function well as pointers.

✔ Compile scrapbooks as records of class activities during the year. Include a photograph of the entire class, individual pictures, drawings, special honors awarded to each child, and newspaper clippings featuring members of the class.

✔ On designated days let the students publicize their favorite television characters. They can make masks and hats to wear, and the more ambitious pupils can make simple costumes. Set up a poll to indicate which character is best liked by the largest number of people. Suggest that the class members make posters or sandwich boards on which original commercials for special programs are displayed.

✔ Schedule an occasional overnight campout in the classroom itself. Serve evening snacks that have been prepared by the children during the day. Take a night walk to explore the night sky and sounds of the evening. Let each child bring his own sleeping equipment.   ✔ Also, extend an invitation to small groups of children to visit your own home for a brief visit from time to time.

✔ You can sharpen the children's sense of history by burying a time capsule in the fall and digging it up again in the spring. Include in the capsule pictures drawn by the pupils and examples of their handwriting and other work that can readily be compared to their later work. Include also a set of the general goals for the year as well as pupils' predictions concerning what events will likely have happened during the intervening months.

✔ Encourage good citizenship by sharing freely with other people in the community. Prepare songs, poems, stories, and pictures to exchange with other classes in the school or with other schools in the district.   ✔ Other professionals listed in education journals can be asked to set up an interchange of letters and art projects.   ✔ Present special programs for parents and other members of the community.   ✔ Take a trip to a children's home or a nursing home.   ✔ If a telephone or a tape recorder is handy, use it to communicate with people who are confined to their homes. Students enjoy interaction with people outside the school.

✔ When children are forgetful, make a treasure box for all items that have been left out of place. Ask children to ransom their possessions by answering a simple cognitive question or by performing some simple stunt.

✔ Brighten up the winter by celebrating January as "Blah Month." Post prominently in the room a large replica of a calendar with lift-up flaps under each of which is written a special event for just that one day. Each morning during the month ask a different child to unloosen the seal covering that day's flap to tell the class the treat that is in store for them.

✔ Set up one area of the room to be used only for spare time amusement. This spot might be labeled the "Fun House." Furnish this center with very interesting materials, including toys, games, puzzles, comics, and cartoons. Add the element of surprise by also having a grab bag filled with minor treats or cards on which special activities are listed.

Handling Punishments

Even the most effective teacher in the most efficient classroom sometimes has children who need to be punished. Punishment that is reasonable and humane helps children realize that there are consequences for all human behaviors in a democratic society. If a citizen breaks the law, there is a penalty to pay. However, when it does become necessary to punish a child, it is possible to offer justice to the miscreant while protecting the integrity of the democratic process. ✔ Class members, if they are adequately mature, may be allowed to discuss the distribution of punishments for minor infractions of the general social contract just as long as all members of the group have sufficiently participated in the formation of the contract and understand all stipulations of the agreements. It is important that the teacher reserve the right to overrule any class-developed penalty that is too severe. When there is no specific punishment mentioned in the communal documents, a child may be allowed to choose a form of chastening that he thinks is in keeping with the misdeed.

Should it become necessary for the teacher to reprimand children and issue punishments to them, several suggestions can make the task more pleasant and effective.

✔ Do not expect a child to apologize for his misdemeanors. Making a child publicly state "I'm sorry" is only to humiliate him, break his spirit, or force him to submit to the power of the teacher or the pressure of his peers. If a child is truly sorry for his mistake, he may be encouraged to show his regrets; but if he is not sorry, a forced apology is likely only to develop resentment and resistance.

✔ Avoid either blaming children for misconduct or shaming them into good behavior. However poorly implemented a child's judgment may be, his motives should not be questioned. Be especially careful not to compare one child with any other child in an effort to shape good conduct. Using one student as a model is unfair both to the child and to his classmates. Children soon learn to resent those students whose behaviors are held up for others to emulate.

✔ When criticizing a child's behavior, respect his need for privacy and confidentiality. Try to admonish children when there is no audience present. Refrain from sharing the content of such a discussion with the other members of the class. Make an effort to criticize the behavior instead of the child himself.

✔ Resort to a variety of reasonable punishments as they are needed, and try to connect them logically with the error being corrected. The child who willfully damages someone's property ought to be expected to reimburse the expense, while the pupil who makes a careless clutter should be asked to clean it up.

✔ Administer punishments only for short, well-defined periods of time. Encourage the child to help decide what a reasonable period might be. Have available in the classroom a simple kitchen timer which can be set to remind the child how long a certain type of punishment might last.

✔ Corporal punishment is not appropriate in the open classroom, for it shows the children that the ultimate solution of problems by adults rests in their power and authority. Striking a child is a contradiction of the need to solve problems through reasonable discussion. In rare instances it may be necessary physically to remove a child from a situation of conflict or to restrain him from hurting another child or harming himself; however, a teacher should not strike a child.

✔ Think of other members of the professional staff as sources of assistance when a child needs intensive help. Look upon all faculty as members of the entire team. Refrain from using the school principal as the chief disciplinarian. Threats such as "If you don't behave I'll send you to the office!" only portray the office as some type of penal enclosure and the principal as chief-ogre-in-residence. Seek out those persons on the staff who have had special training in counseling or in teaching methods. Discover the agencies in the community that have something to offer disturbed children.

✔ Be sure to work closely with the parents of children in trouble. Approach them as potential sources of information that may assist in the solution of difficulties. Assume that parents are equally concerned for the welfare of their children, even if parents' values and methods differ widely from your own. Present children's problems not as a series of complaints but as a type of inquiry into causative factors.

chapter ten
Evaluating the Success of the Open Approach

Accountability and Evaluation

The idea that teachers should be accountable for the results of their efforts in classrooms is certainly not a new one. To the degree that all teachers are informally compared one with another by parents and children every day, they are indeed being evaluated. Whenever principals make judgments about tenure and promotions, accountability is at work. Wherever any form of merit pay is under consideration, accountability enters into the decision.

Recently, however, the use of more formal accountability procedures has emerged as a national issue in education. Performance contracting offered to students, competency-based training provided for teachers, behavioral objectives for all types of learners, and the demands of tax-burdened communities have all contributed to the desire for evidence of a fair dollar's worth of teaching. Unfortunately for children, many educators believe that assessment of teaching merely involves identifying specific behavioral objectives, then teaching for those goals, and finally, testing to see how much learning has occurred. This somewhat simplistic view of accountability unhappily encourages teachers to teach only for the tests that are administered, and it likewise tends to turn children into subject matter technicians because technical information and skills are most easily taught and most easily identified on a test instrument. If the child discovers that the only real value of attending school is to acquire just enough information to pass tests and thereby get out of school, there is little hope that he will ever appreciate the real merit of the subjects being taught. Scientific inquiry, for example, is much more than the acquisition of a set of formulae; mathematics involves more than a collection of operations and number facts; good reading requires attitudes and insights. Although factual information is an important part of every area of the curriculum, transmission of these bits of data should not be the primary goal of a school mainly because factual information is always changing. What are facts today may become fiction tomorrow; the improbable of this moment becomes reality in only a few years. Even seemingly irrefutable facts are often subject to argument. The question "Who discovered America?" no longer has only one answer. In fact, it is far more important to explore with children answers to the query "*Why* was America discovered?"

This de-emphasis of factual information does not become an exclusion of such information in a responsible open instructional program. Every child must learn to compute, and every child also needs to write accurately and clearly. However, in the open classroom the teacher focuses on specific information required by students in identified learning situations. She does not misuse the time of those who have already mastered those same facts by requiring all students to experience the same learning activities. Furthermore, the open teacher stresses the development of generalizations and the acquisition of information through exploration of interesting materials and through firsthand experiences, rather than through rote repetition. The child who sees logic and relationships in his studies is more likely to remember the factual data that he encounters every day.

New Roles for Testing and Other Assessments

Another difference between evaluation procedures found in the open classroom and in the traditional classroom involves testing. In the conventional classroom testing plays a significant role because it is often on the basis of test results that a child is placed in an ability group or even promoted from one grade to another. Testing is also done extensively during the instructional week in traditional settings, for the instructor tends to teach a concept or skill to a large group of children and then to test their mastery of the items she thinks are a fair sample of what she has taught. If the class demonstrates an adequate level of competency, the teacher moves on to a new set of skills. Those students who did not perform well on tests are offered added practice or are directed to remedial materials. The teacher interprets the results of her tests in the form of grades and averages, with special emphasis on how well each child has performed in the light of grade-level expectations.

In the open classroom the child assumes the main responsibility for evaluating his progress. He keeps his own records, he confers personally and frequently with the teacher, and he plans subsequent learning activities to meet the needs that he and his teacher jointly identify. He checks the accuracy of his work as soon as it is done. Testing, as such, is minimized. However, when testing is appropriate to open learning, the teacher offers her children the option of taking tests for which they are comfortably ready. Tests are used as further learning opportunities because each detected deficiency leads to a greater degree of mastery. At times different children may be taking different tests, as in the case of a unit test on programmed material or a Friday afternoon spelling test on personalized lists of words.

In open classrooms test results are not used as discriminators and therefore are not likely to cause anxieties among the students. The evaluation of the child, whether it be done by the learner or by the teacher, is effected in terms of the individual's own needs, interests, and abilities. The element of competition, so commonplace in traditional classrooms, is dramatically changed, for instead of competing against other children, the open learner is challenged to better his own previous effort and to move his goals farther along as his proficiency in a subject area improves. The open teacher stresses general competency rather than perfection, for she helps each child to set objectives that are in keeping with his self-concept, his past experiences, and his capabilities. One child may be able to spell twenty new words each week, but another child may be able to handle only ten. One student may reasonably be expected to work 100% of his mathematics problems correctly, but another pupil might be encouraged to aim for only 70% accuracy.

Still another difference in open evaluation lies in the fact that there is much less interrogation by the teacher than usually occurs in conventional classrooms. Consider, for example, the traditional primary grades reading circle where the teacher often directs a torrent of questions at the group. Since every paragraph that is read has its inevitable queries, the child soon learns to read only to find the correct responses, rather than to enjoy the events in the story. Similarly, in the traditional setting every book taken out of the library must be reported on; every piece of homework must be corrected; every written composition must be red-penciled; every field trip requires a class discussion or a written reaction. In such a situation there is very little likelihood of learning just for the sake of knowing something, or learning simply because either the process or the content is something interesting and enjoyable. When questioning is done in the open classroom, it occurs only to the extent that it tells the teacher what the child needs further to know. Queries are significant and probing and personalized. The child is permitted to decide which method is most useful in reporting: for example, there is no need for him to present before the class the inevitable oral book report when there are available at least fifty alternative reporting activities from which he might select a more interesting approach.

One other difference between open and conventional evaluation is that open assessment is more likely to be continuous and immediate. In the traditional situation the student completes his assignment and then turns it in for checking. If he has made a major error in his work, he may have to wait a day or more to discover his mistake; in contrast, the open learner checks his own work right away and avoids the necessity for rethinking and relearning what he has just experienced. No longer must he laboriously recopy his spelling words, rework his math problems, or rewrite his compositions. The teacher is freed of her job of ferreting out errors because the student can provide his own correction much more efficiently than can even the most conscientious teacher, and in so doing he saves the teacher valuable time and provides a constant monitor on his own understanding.

Grading Pupil Progress and Reporting to Parents

It is all too easy for parents to insist on traditional grading procedures and report cards. After all, most contemporary parents were themselves evaluated in that very way, and there is something comforting about a reporting system that is both familiar and easy to understand. Further, there is always a kind of proprietary interest parents have in examining their child's report card, either to note the high grades and compare them with those of the neighbors' children, or else to use the number of low grades as a threat against their own offspring who are not performing up to the teachers' expectations.

However, a close look at report cards reveals several inadequacies, the first and most obvious of which is that the report card gives very little useful information. To think that an entire six- or nine-weeks period could be distilled into a cluster of grades written on a piece of paper is almost unthinkable; yet it is done nationwide every year in millions of cases.

A second failing of report cards is the wide variance in the computation of the grades themselves. Classic research studies reveal that grading practices differ widely from teacher to teacher: what one teacher terms a "C" effort another teacher labels an "A." It is no wonder that many parents are confused when their children move from grade to grade or from one subject specialist to another. All sorts of variables are included in traditional grades. One teacher may judge a student on statistical evidence alone, clinging to an artificial and arbitrary scale on which 70 percent is passing regardless of the adequacy of the teaching or the appropriateness of the assessment instrument; another teacher, impressed with a child's effort or swayed by the probable impact of her grading on a child's morale, may lower or raise his grade accordingly; still another teacher may be influenced by a pupil's personality or by his behavior in the classroom.

A third important consideration involves the student's self-concept. In the traditional school only a select few students earn honors, while the majority of pupils never attain high levels of achievement and thus are rarely recognized. The child who receives from school an official document that time after time labels him as "mediocre" or as a "failure" can only be expected to live in keeping with this judgment. The student who is identified as a "poor achiever" or as a "slow student" tends to think of himself in that way and performs correspondingly. Of course there is no need to try to fool children concerning their abilities; in truth, children need to have a fair idea of how their capabilities compare with their peers', but this realistic appraisal generally comes as the result of informal interactions with their classmates. Most children in a classroom know which student is outstanding in science, which one is the fastest runner, which one is clever at solving arithmetic problems, and which one is gifted in drawing pictures of horses. Any perceptive child knows fairly well where he stands in his group; there is really no need to confirm his thinking with grades on report cards that suggest, in essence, that his teacher agrees with his assessment and that of his classmates.

Ideally the open teacher should be able to dispense with the traditional report cards and grading procedures that are found in most American schools. However, open teachers working in conventional schools may be required to issue some type of formal reporting device. If written reporting is mandatory, the open teacher may be able to reconcile the interests of her parents with the needs of her pupils by offering grades on a somewhat different basis. ✔ One possibility is to offer a child a stipulated grade for the satisfactory completion of a contract to which the child has earlier agreed; by designating an appropriate number of projects to complete, a number of points to accumulate, or a level of competency to attain, the contract approach can give a measure of satisfaction to pupil and parent alike. Such a contract can combine points for both the quantity of the work and the quality of work because the teacher awards bonus credit for effort and achievement that is beyond expectation. ✔ Other variations of newer reporting procedures are to develop an original report card that records anecdotal remarks and to invent a checklist on which specific skills are noted. Such a collection of specific behaviors and learning outcomes can be further categorized with notations such as "easy for most fifth graders." Somewhere on a checklist indicate the number of children in the room who have already mastered specific tasks (Figure 44), or provide boxes for checking the degree of involvement in the tasks: "Learning" suggests that the child is just becoming involved in the concept; "Competent" shows that the child has attained an adequate level of achievement; "Mastered" indicates that the child is completely confident in the indicated area (Figure 45). Color code these boxes like an athletic scorecard to further maintain pupil interest.

In the same schools where formal grading is commonplace, honors assemblies, honor rolls, and honor certificates are also an important part of the rewards system. Unhappily for most pupils the same children tend to be honored year after year, with the same names regularly appearing on the honor roll. The students who may need no such external motivation to help them achieve their goals are thereby publicly recognized, while the much larger proportion of the student body who might conceivably benefit from such public recognition rarely receives it. The further unfairness of such reinforcement is demonstrated by the fact that the less able child may in fact be expending much greater effort than do his more talented classmates.

✔ To provide the kind of visible acclaim that all children enjoy, develop a more personalized approach. Designate general categories of accomplishment: "Notable Improvement," "Outstanding Progress," and "Superior Effort" are a few examples of compliments that can be offered at some time or other to just about every child in the classroom. To provide even further visible support, invent a variety of certificates from bond paper, satin ribbons and notarial seals. At the conclusion of each grading period identify each person's most notable characteristic, his best achievement, or his greatest contribution to the group. In this manner every pupil in the room can be given at least one document as proof that his time in school was well spent. Teachers must demonstrate that steady growth and per-

YOUR CHILD, *Janet* , CAN DO THE THINGS
MARKED WITH ✔. THE NUMBER OF (<u>HER</u> - HIS)
CLASSMATES WHO ALSO CAN DO THEM IS IN THE
RIGHTHAND COLUMN.

TIE OWN SHOES	✔	23
USE A HANDKERCHIEF	✔	21
CATCH A LARGE BALL	✔	19
COUNT BY ONES TO 20	✔	20
COUNT BY FIVES TO 100		6
CUT WITH SCISSORS		17
RECOGNIZE ALL CAPITAL LETTERS	✔	22
RECOGNIZE ALL SMALL LETTERS		4
KNOW EIGHT BASIC COLORS	✔	23
CARRY SIMPLE MELODY		14
KNOW LEFT FROM RIGHT	✔	17

COMMENTS:

Could use practice with cutting.
Follows directions well.
Creative in art activities.
Likes to make up own songs.
Sometimes forgets to wait turn.

Figure 44 Personal Skills Checklist

Figure 45 Checklist Report

Mathematics Report

Symbols Code: Student:

E = Easy for most fifth graders
A = Average difficulty for most fifth graders
H = Hard for most fifth graders

L (Learning)   = has just begun working with concept or skill
C (Competent)   = is experienced, but makes occasional errors
M (Mastery)   = is comfortable, makes no errors in process

		Nov. 1	Jan. 8	Apr. 9	Jun. 6
Finding perimeter of squares	E	M	M	M	M
Dividing two digits by one digit	E	M	M	M	M
Converting even numerals to factors	A	L	C	M	M
Multiplying through the 6 times table	E	M	M	M	M
Dividing with 2-digit divisor	A	L	C	C	M
Using metric linear measurement	A	L	C	M	M
Understanding distributive property	A		L	C	M
Multiplying through the 9 times table	A	L	L	C	C
Finding areas of square, triangle	A	L	C	M	M
Knowing terms relating to circles	A	M	M	M	M
Finding volume of cube	A	L	M	M	M
Adding and subtracting with decimals	H				L
Understanding ratio and proportion	H			L	L
Multiplying improper fractions	H			L	C

COMMENTS:

Bill has worked independently on Base 2 and is making a model of a computer.

sonal satisfaction of the students are at least as important as winning the top academic honors in any subject area (Figure 46).

In the open classroom parents are involved in planning the program and are informed about the teacher's success with their children. Probably the best means of reporting to parents, and one that can either supplant or supplement the written report, is the parent-teacher conference. Much more can be exchanged in a series of thirty-minute encounters than can ever be conveyed on even the best report card. Such personal contacts should occur often enough for the parents to become acquainted with the teacher's professional and human qualities. The purpose of such conferences should be to provide information to parent and teacher alike. "What can you teach me about your child?" should be the most important question posed by the professional, for every parent has much information about

Figure 46   Personalized Awards

his or her child. ✔ For her contribution to parent conferences the teacher needs to be adequately prepared with typical work produced by each child, with a record of pupil progress, and with questions soliciting parents' suggestions for improving the instructional program. ✔ If parents seem reluctant to come to school for such discussions, offer to visit parents in their homes or propose a "neutral" location such as a local coffee shop. Summarize each oral encounter with a brief written comment on the main points mentioned, and suggest a definite date either for a subsequent conference or for a follow-up telephone call when a child needs added assistance at home.

Another way to include parents in informal evaluation is to invite them to visit the classroom often enough to observe firsthand the variety of activities available in the open room, to examine the materials children are using, to see the degree of structure the open approach requires, and to note the general continuity from month to month. After noticing how their own children interact with other children in the classroom, and how they perform on their daily tasks, parents are much better able to make judgments about their children's progress in school. ✔ As a part of the parent-teacher cooperative evaluation, offer questionnaires on which parents are able to assess their children's responses at home as well as at school. If the open approach is truly effective, there are many constructive behaviors that students should practice in their homes and communities. Parental evaluation forms not only collect information for the teacher but also help sensitize parents to the important goals of the open approach (Figure 47). Also offer to parents an end-of-year opportunity to evaluate teaching competencies and to make suggestions for greater professional growth (Figure 48).

Solving Problems of Promotions and Transitions

In the school building where there are found open classrooms at more than one grade level, the matter of promotion is not particularly relevant because children can move easily from one open group to a similar one the following year. They may even be permitted to remain with the same teacher for two or three years. In such situations grade level promotions are not important, for in the open setting practices such as retaining children in the same grade or skipping a child by double-promoting him need not be considered as appropriate. If the child is progressing in an open classroom at a pace that is consistent with his own abilities, and if he is motivated to learn because his interests are adequately reflected in the curriculum, then nothing further should be expected of him. Comments such as "Socially immature," "Small for his age," and "Just not ready for promotion" have no place on the records of children in open schools. The open teacher looks upon variations as not only inevitable but desirable, and her success in teaching should be measured in part by the extent to which this ever-widening range of charac-

Figure 47   Parental Pupil Evaluation

PARENTS:

Please take a few minutes to help us find out how your child has responded to school this year. You need not sign your name unless you choose to do so.

YES NO

☐☐ Is your child more interested in school this year than in past years?

☐☐ Has your child developed any new interests recently?

☐☐ Does your child express general satisfaction with his/her achievements in school?

☐☐ Does your child usually look forward to coming to school?

☐☐ Does your child freely share with you the things he has learned?

☐☐ Is your child able to apply at home the things he has discovered in class?

☐☐ Have the school-related habits of your child improved this year (think of examples such as remembering good rules of safety, taking better care of his/her body, reading more books at home)?

☐☐ Do you think your child is under less pressure to achieve?

☐☐ Does your child have more self-confidence?

☐☐ Is your child more willing to start new activities?

☐☐ Is your child more resourceful in solving his/her own problems involving others who are his age?

☐☐ Is your child more sensitive to and tolerant of others?

☐☐ Does your child express more curiosity about the world and ask more questions concerning things he doesn't understand?

☐☐ Is your child better motivated to study at home?

Figure 48   Parental Teacher Evaluation

PARENTS:

In order to make my teaching next year more effective, I would appreciate your open and honest responses to any or all of these questions. You need not sign your name. You may send the survey back with your child who will place it in a box outside our classroom door.

YES NO

☐☐ Do I seem to be responsive to the emotional and social needs of your child?

☐☐ Do I appear to respect your child as a human being?

☐☐ Am I adequately knowledgeable in the various areas of the curriculum?

☐☐ Have I provided an appropriate variety of learning materials and media for the students?

☐☐ Is my classroom interesting to the students?

☐☐ Do the classroom activities seem to be useful and relevant to your child?

☐☐ Have I reported your child's progress adequately?

☐☐ Do you feel free to visit my classroom?

☐☐ Has your child made any suggestions that I might benefit from?

☐☐ Has your child gained adequately in intellectual growth this year?

☐☐ Would you want to have your child in my classroom another year?

☐☐ Do you have any questions about my procedures that I should answer in greater detail?

teristics increases while children are in her care. Whenever a child is held back in a grade or is double-promoted, or if he fails a subject, there is a strong suggestion that the school was in some significant way not ready to meet his needs.

The moving of children from an open classroom to a traditional one the following year may represent more of a challenge. One objection to openness is that children might not be able to adjust to a teacher-dominated program after having experienced a pupil-centered year of instruction. The most obvious reply to this objection is that it would not be fair to deprive children of any worthwhile experience just because it might never be repeated; certainly any helpful and supportive contact with an open teacher can be justified on its own merits. A second reply to the objection is that children's very role as students, even in traditional schools, requires them to adjust from year to year to many different teachers. Fortunately children by nature are generally much more resilient than adults and find the process of adjustment relatively simple to handle. A final point to mention is that children trained in open classrooms should be unusually able to adapt to changing circumstances; adaptability, flexibility, and problem solving skills are all important elements in the open approach, and if the open teacher has done her job well, her students should be able to accommodate any new expectations confronting them. Of course the open teacher does her children a service by communicating with other professionals in the school so that they will have a clearer understanding of what she has attempted to do with her pupils during the year. The open teacher also owes to other teachers complete information concerning each child she has taught. Such data include lists of skills mastered, samples of pupil work, self-evaluations prepared by the students themselves, copies of reporting documents, and significant anecdotal records.

Self-Reporting by Students

Besides the report cards, conferences, and questionnaires which provide communication between teachers and parents, there are assessment items that show how the child himself perceives his success and that allow him to share his studies with other members of the class.

✔ Allow the children to make up their own tests, which might be something as simple as a set of comprehension questions at the end of a story or a review of an entire unit of study. Tests made by students not only help the children to realize that their involvement in evaluation is important, but these tests also tell the teacher what the class learned from an activity and what they thought were the essential elements of the exercise.

✔ Encourage each successive child who uses a set of materials to contribute one new discovery to a collection accruing on a set of fact cards filed in a recipe box. Such bits of information can be organized in the form of a game so that children can check comprehension while they are having fun reviewing the concepts.

✔ A personal diary or log can be maintained by each child, who adds brief comments to it at the end of each day's session. Instruct each student to enumerate the major activities he has undertaken and to identify his main studies (Figure 49). ✔ Ask him to choose from his projects and products of the day the ones that give him the most pride. ✔ Suggest that each child maintain in a small spiral notebook personal notes that might serve as a sort of a passport between home and school. In this way parents are also informed of their children's daily progress. ✔ Some children might prefer to draw a daily cartoon or comic strip of their classroom involvements.

✔ Other forms of self-assessment might include a scrapbook in which are kept outstanding examples of student work selected by each child in the group. ✔ Encourage some students to establish a checklist or a section in a notebook on which they list their accomplishments under headings such as "I Can

Record Main Studies on 3 x 5 cards and Hang Them on hooks. Take them home Fridays.	MAR. 3	MAR. 4	MAR. 5	MAR. 6	MAR. 7
JACKIE	·	·	·	·	·
JILL	·	·	·	·	·
JONAS	·	·	·	·	·
LAURA		·	·	·	·
LOUIS					
NANCY	·	·	·	·	
PAULA	·	·	·	·	·
ROGER	·	·	·	·	·
SALLY	·	·	·	·	·
SERENA	·	·	·	·	·
SUSAN	·	·	·	·	·
TOMMY	·		·	·	·
TYRONE	·	·	·	·	·
VAL	·	·	·	·	·

Figure 49   Personal Progress Log

Do This," or "Things I Know."   ✔ A variation of this idea is the use of a series of colorful cans labeled "I *Can* Can." Allow each child to deposit slips of paper in appropriate cans; on the slips of paper have the contributor write each major achievement as it occurs. This technique and other self-assessment devices are illustrated in Figures 50 and 51.

✔ A different end-of-day assessment technique is some form of sharing time when each child is allowed to show his peers what he has accomplished during the session. This might take place as a "Show Me" period when several groups of children are distributed about the classroom for simple demonstrations. One test of a child's learning is his ability to explain what he knows to someone else at his own level.

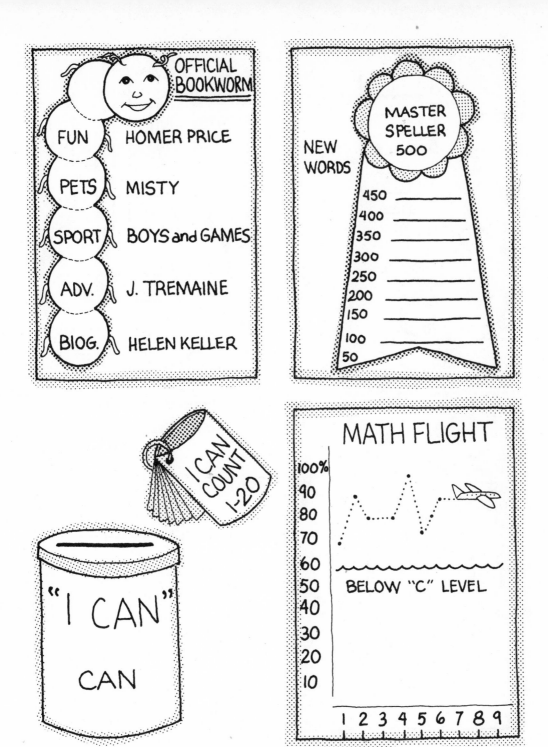

Figure 50   Self-Assessment Devices

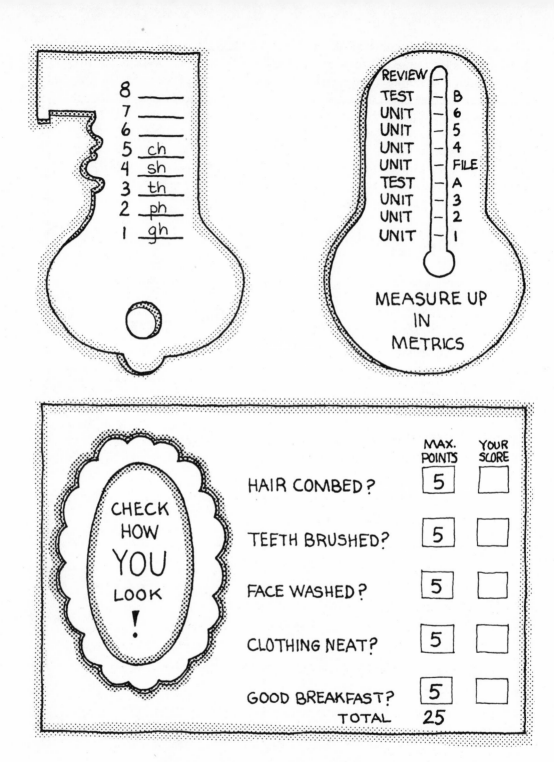

Figure 51   Self-Assessment Devices

✔ Set up a simple teacher evaluation form which solicits children's perceptions and feelings on a checklist or a rating scale (Figure 52). If a child is too young to read such a document, read each item aloud and ask him to circle the appropriate face that reflects his judgments (Figure 53). ✔ As a further inquiry into feelings, schedule frequent discussions during which children are encouraged to air their compliments and their complaints. ✔ For those pupils who are less likely to engage in such an exchange, set up in the room a "Gripe Box" or a "Gr-r-r-eat Box" into which pupils may drop slips of paper on which they have written either positive or negative reactions to things that have happened in the group.

Figure 52   Students' Teacher-Evaluation Form

STUDENTS:

You will help me become a better teacher by giving an honest reply to these statements. Please mark the boxes that best show how you feel. You are not required to sign your name.

☐ I really enjoy being in this class.

☐ I think I am learning a lot.

☐ My teacher respects me as a person.

☐ My teacher listens to the students in this class.

☐ My assignments are interesting and useful.

☐ The students help each other learn.

☐ My teacher treats me fairly.

☐ My teacher likes to teach.

☐ My teacher explains hard things well.

☐ I don't mind making mistakes.

☐ My teacher is reasonable in the work that is required.

☐ My teacher has a sense of humor.

☐ My teacher doesn't mind admitting errors.

☐ I can see the connection between different subjects.

☐ I have a lot to say about how, when, and where I do my learning.

☐ My teacher encourages students to bring up different ideas.

☐ My teacher is sensitive to my feelings.

☐ I look forward to coming to school each day.

☐ I can use materials in ways that are different from those suggested by the teacher.

☐ I would like to have my teacher again next year.

Figure 53   Prereaders' Teacher-Evaluation Form

PUPILS: Circle the face that best shows how you feel about each item.

1. ☺ ☹ ☹ Coming to school is fun.
2. ☺ ☹ ☹ This year has been a good one for me.
3. ☺ ☹ ☹ I have lots of friends in this room.
4. ☺ ☹ ☹ My teacher really likes me.
5. ☺ ☹ ☹ This classroom looks nice.
6. ☺ ☹ ☹ I like to study about science.
7. ☺ ☹ ☹ This shows how I feel about story books.
8. ☺ ☹ ☹ My teacher is fair to everybody.
9. ☺ ☹ ☹ I have really tried hard this year.
10. ☺ ☹ ☹ I do all right in number work.
11. ☺ ☹ ☹ My teacher trusts me.
12. ☺ ☹ ☹ I enjoy being a helper in the room.
13. ☺ ☹ ☹ Most people in this class are nice to me.
14. ☺ ☹ ☹ My favorite time is recess.
15. ☺ ☹ ☹ I am good at lots of things.
16. ☺ ☹ ☹ I wish I had more homework to do.
17. ☺ ☹ ☹ I enjoy running and jumping.
18. ☺ ☹ ☹ I look forward to art and music.
19. ☺ ☹ ☹ My teacher listens to what I say.
20. ☺ ☹ ☹ I have fun with words.
21. ☺ ☹ ☹ I get to decide things about how I should act.
22. ☺ ☹ ☹ I usually behave myself in school.
23. ☺ ☹ ☹ Learning new things is interesting.

Research and Open Education

When thinking about open education, one might naturally ask "What does responsible research suggest that would neither confirm or refute the claims made for the open approach?" The answer to this simple query is not easy to find. For one thing, even under the most carefully controlled circumstances collecting information through testing does not guarantee the truth or the usefulness of the results. Any teacher experienced in testing is well aware of the problems that often contaminate data collected through standardized measurement: children may be less alert either early in the morning or late in the day; children may not be feeling well; some students experience stress and anxiety in any test situation; certain events occurring outside the classroom may distract pupils from their tasks. Further, even when tests include both a control group and an experimental group, there is often present a halo effect that confuses the issue. There are so many intangible qualities present in teaching and in testing that it is difficult at best to prove a point by amassing technical data based on children's performances that are assessed in this brief way.

Another challenge confronting research on open education has to do with the investigator's approach to teaching. There are some professionals who think of education as a science defined in closely written behavioral objectives and expressed in terms of competency-based criteria. When this philosophy is accepted by the researcher, the collection of technical information is a relatively simple matter. However, when the inquirer approaches teaching as an art, there is very little tangible evidence to accumulate. If elements such as sensitivity to children, attitudes about teaching, and dedication to tasks are discussed, perhaps the work produced by the children is more compelling substantiation of the efficacy of a teaching style than is technical data.

A final difficulty in validating open education lies in the matter of terminology. A number of reported research studies have investigated comparative intellectual achievements of children in "open space" classrooms and those working in "closed space" classrooms. As discussed in Chapter 2, "Open space" is not a synonym for "open education," and open space is not even an essential part of the open approach. Furthermore, the testing done in such limited research efforts is often intended to assess only academic achievement; this intention manifestly misses the point of the open approach because the real purpose of open education is not to prepare scholars but to produce learners. If a fair job is to be done in such investigations, the researchers need to evaluate how well the children handle the basic processes and tools of learning. Questions like these are significant in such an effort:

- ☐ Do the children show more initiative in finding their own answers to questions?
- ☐ Do the children have a strong sense of inquiry and curiosity?
- ☐ Do the children approach their tasks independently?
- ☐ Do the children have better attitudes about school?
- ☐ Are the children original in their thinking?
- ☐ Are the children eager to explore new materials?
- ☐ Can the children solve their own personal problems?
- ☐ Is there greater fluency of expression in the classroom?

In another vein, the research might also explore interpersonal relationships because the social and emotional development of the child in the open setting is at least as important as his academic prowess. Questions such as the following might produce interesting responses:

- ☐ Is there usually a cooperative and sharing spirit in the room?
- ☐ Are the children more sensitive to the needs of others?
- ☐ Can the children generally govern their own behavior?
- ☐ Do the children respect the rights of other class members?
- ☐ Do the children accept the individual differences represented in the student population?
- ☐ Are children more careful about the use of their equipment and furniture?
- ☐ Have the parents shown a greater interest in the school?
- ☐ Have the children been better able to settle their personal difficulties?

Although the task of researching open education is a difficult one, and although only a few limited studies have as yet been produced, there is some evidence from several responsible sources that children in open settings generally hold their own in academic achievement comparisons with students in traditional classrooms. Furthermore, several research studies have also indicated a tendency for children in open classrooms to show a greater ability to study independently, produce a wider variety of creative products, demonstrate more resourcefulness in solving problems, exhibit more curiosity, and display better insights in certain social relationships.

Of course such evidence is fragmentary. Much research remains to be done; it is hoped that investigators will discover answers to questions raised about open education by critics and friends alike. However, it is important that the classroom teacher not wait until the validity and usefulness of open education is "proved" through statistical analysis. Because dispute and argument characterize most of the important theories of instruction, open education will likely remain a controversial topic regardless of the nature of the research data collected. If a teacher believes in the soundness of the principles of open education, it is essential for her to choose at least one useful idea and try to make it work in her own classroom. If, in the course of her teaching, she discovers that her children are glad to come to school, happy to work on their tasks, and reluctant to leave when school is done, she will have at least a measure of assurance that the open approach can accomplish much of what is claimed on its behalf.

chapter eleven
Providing Professional Resources

Establishing Teacher Centers

One of the more useful outgrowths of the open movement in England has been the establishment of teacher centers throughout the country. A teacher center is a room or a building that is central to the professionals in a district or a region and that has specifically been set aside to serve their instructional needs. Some of these centers in England are supported by the Local Education Authority, the counterpart of the American board of education, but in other instances the center is funded entirely by local subscription of the persons using it. If large numbers of teachers visit any single center, the English hire a warden to supervise its use and, at times, to provide in-service assistance.

The development of teacher centers in American schools has great potential for involving both open teachers and their administrators in a team effort. Such a facility should model the design of classroom learning centers, and the same goals used in open settings should be replicated in teacher centers. Teacher centers should be located where many different materials are accumulated, where there is space for planning and preparation, and where people can interact in a mutually supportive relationship. Containers for supplies, tools, scrap items, equipment, and instructional aids should be clearly labeled, and the responsibilities for care of the area should be made clear.

Actual locations for teacher centers depend on what is available in schools. In communities with declining student populations some buildings have vacant classrooms; even empty schools are a possibility. ✔ Where nothing better is available, a large storage closet can be cleaned, decorated, and converted into a mini-center. ✔ Another choice is to change a substantial portion of a central library into a teacher center. ✔ If no such spot is available, an alternate course of action is to make or purchase a set of wheeled carts that can be loaded with permanent equipment and supplies, moved from room to room, and stored under a stairwell or along a hall.

The most obvious activities that might occur in a teacher center relate to the development of instructional aids for classroom use. For this purpose the center should be equipped with all the items, consumable and permanent, that are needed for the job. ✔ In addition, the center can serve as the central location of periodicals and books that are the sources of ideas for games, puzzles, devices, worksheets, and other objects of learning. ✔ To provide even greater help, identify each teacher's areas of expertise and special interest; include information about hobbies, travel experiences, and professional background in a booklet that also contains data about adult members of the community who have an interest in supplementing and supporting the instructional program.

✔ Another important function for the teacher center team is to provide in-service leadership not only in general teaching methods, but more specially in explaining the options available in the open approach. Collections of professional literature on openness can contribute greatly to a better understanding of the subject. The teacher center can serve as a seminar spot for student teachers and as a locus for training provided by colleagues from other schools in the district or from colleges and universities. More ambitious members of the open staff may want to develop newsletters to be exchanged with instructors in other classrooms. The rental of films on this important topic is still another opportunity for those committed to the concepts of open education.

✔ Finally, the teacher center might also be used as a social club providing an informal atmosphere for pupils, parents, and professionals alike. Where it is appropriate, such a center might be open occasional evenings or Saturday mornings for communal efforts in preparing puppet shows, readying foods for a party or a picnic, working on crafts or other hobbies, or constructing play equipment, learning aids, and other items more closely related to the classroom program.

In days of tightening school budgets, such a center need not be expensive, although many administrators and families have elected to include expenses of the center in the regular commitments of communities. ✔ An alternate source of funding is a local parent-teacher organization; in many localities such a group is involved in fund-raising projects during the year, and the establishing and support of a teacher center serving both school personnel and families is a unique and easily identified recipient of such efforts. If such an arrangement is not possible, the teachers in the school may decide upon some form of voluntary self-assessment whereby minor funds are raised to take care of expenditures for consumable materials or inexpensive pieces of permanent equipment.

Converting Libraries into Learning Sites

In schools where the open approach is popularly supported by most of the professional staff, there is an opportunity to change the function of the traditional library into a media center that more effectively serves the needs of self-directed learners.

An important element in this process of conversion is the job of the librarian herself. No longer is the librarian mainly a cataloging specialist and a custodian of shelves of books. In the open school the librarian must become instead a media specialist trained in the acquisition of all types of communication devices besides the conventional books, pamphlets, and newspapers; filmstrips, records, pictures, learning kits, film loops, films, and tape cassettes are only a few of the possible supplementary sources of information. But the mere acquisition of such items is not sufficient in itself, for the media specialist must know how to operate such devices, must know how best to find information using each one, and must be able to show children and teachers how to prepare their own learning materials.

A second difference between the open and the conventional library is the physical management of space and materials. By centralizing present collections of media and by consolidating subsequent purchases, the media specialist reduces duplication and makes her expenditures more efficient. Further, the ready access to the media center by children from open classrooms strongly suggests that the librarian-turned-specialist must be available for children arriving at all hours of the instructional day and must not insist on the traditional once-weekly visit by large groups of children; pupils working in and out of open classrooms will assign their own work and will sign in and sign out of classrooms and libraries with increasing freedom. Management techniques must also change; the concept of the library-media center as a hushed sanctuary for the student must give way to the notion of a center where children can interact in their investigations. Reasonable levels of noise are to be expected in the media center, for control of noise is the responsibility given the child in the open classroom.

Finally, the media center should look like the learning centers found elsewhere in the school. Subdivided into learning stations, the media center needs to feature each piece of equipment and each major resource with its own self-explanatory directions for use. Aides and student helpers should be available to help pupils use the facilities; multiple use of floor space ought to allow for small private study areas as well as large group activities; wall and floor surfaces should be covered with sound absorbent fabrics; furniture and equipment should be flexible and movable; and the decor of the room should be colorful, cheerful, clean, and sufficiently attractive to hold children's attention and to invite them back for subsequent visits.

Finding Resources in the Community

Because one of the tenets of the open approach is that students should encounter important concepts both inside and outside their classrooms, it follows that children should have liberal access to the immediate community. This access should allow large groups, smaller clusters, and individual students to pursue specific kinds of information in field activities. Whatever the size of the learning cluster, it is important that the information gained from a field trip match the resources of the site to be visited. Too often the field activities of traditional classes necessarily require the presence of every child in the class, regardless of his ability to understand and appreciate what is happening. Sometimes such excursions turn into a lark for the class members and a nightmare for the teacher in charge. If individual children are sufficiently mature to handle the responsibility, and if their parents are in informed agreement, those students can be released for a portion of the day to study in the community, on the playground, or in a local park. When a small group of children need to explore a concept together, sets of parents can be enlisted to provide both transportation and supervision.

✔ Make field trips more meaningful by seeing that some kind of permanent record is made on each occasion; photographing the place visited and tape recording children's impressions and the information offered by hosts and guides are both helpful procedures. Encourage the children to share their knowledge with each other through stories, pictures, dramatizations, notebooks, or real objects collected en route. Be careful, however, not to insist on follow-up activities; children should be permitted to believe that learning is its own justification, and a field trip need not generate the inevitable report, drawing, or thank-you letter so often required after traditional classroom excursions.

While thinking of locations for field studies, consider places that are neither spectacular nor far afield. ✔ A simple walk about the school grounds or an examination of a neighbor's garden may produce more learning about the science of plants than would a bus trip to a greenhouse or a farm. Children may get more out of a tour of a local small industry than they receive from an all-day outing to a major airport or a museum. ✔ Community resources also include major pieces of machinery that pass the school from time to time; make arrangements for operators of vehicles such as cement mixers, fire trucks, street sweepers, or bulldozers to stop by the school yard for a few minutes to explain how their equipment operates. ✔ If conditions make it impractical for children to visit field sites, ask the specialists to visit class to demonstrate their expertise; a candy maker, a dancer, a wood carver, a beekeeper, a piano tuner, and a glass blower are just a few examples of community helpers who can be brought to the open classroom.

Collecting Discards and Low-Cost Materials

✔ There are many potential sources of free and inexpensive items that can be incorporated into the instructional program in open classrooms. At the local level, for example, many useful elements are discarded daily by businesses, industries, and other commercial agencies. These materials range from scraps of wood and other building supplies available free of charge from lumber yards to cardboard boxes and decorations salvaged from department stores and groceries. Junk shops and salvage yards can provide machinery and tools, and construction sites are sources of spare bricks, shingles, fiber board, pipe, wire, lumber, and many other supplies. Paper in quantity may be procured from printers, stationery stores, and manufacturers of paper products. In addition, free instructional resources are often available from municipal agencies; most chambers of commerce will supply upon request folders and flyers about local communities and industries. Fraternal organizations and benevolent societies also often disseminate information that can be adapted to the needs of the open classroom.

Beyond the local community the state government furnishes no-cost and low-cost pieces. ✔ Contact, for example, the state department of highways or tourism for road maps and brochures that describe the most interesting features of an area. Ask the state departments of agriculture, forestry, and mines for technical data as well as objects such as seeds, rocks, and plants. Public museums, institutes, and zoos issue free literature, and state departments of education publish pamphlets and curriculum guides for teachers. National organizations are additional sources. Travel clubs and travel agencies prepare maps, posters, pictures, and other information; major automobile manufacturing companies produce historical aids; and trade and professional associations distribute magazines, comics, booklets, and films. Publishers of textbooks for schools offer newsletter privileges, and many of these same companies send out without cost charts, posters, and in-service bulletins. The federal government in Washington, D.C., is another possible source; contact the Superintendent of Public Documents and ask to be placed on the monthly publications mailing list.

Schools themselves are often a source of materials to be recycled in open classrooms. ✔ Check the school office for paper that can be salvaged for student use and contact the shop teachers and home economics teachers for scraps of wood, metal, and fabric to include in crafts programs. Some administrators also have access to government surplus items that are on sale for a small fraction of their original cost.

Requests for low-cost and no-cost supplies are more likely to be granted if they are made in the name of school children. Also, it is good policy to remind people that recycling discarded materials will not only help the students in the classroom but will also spare the environment. ✔ Use official stationery when corresponding with distant agencies, and encourage the pupils to write letters of appreciation. Make a point to acknowledge publicly the contributions of local agencies by writing newsletter articles that are sent home to parents or feature stories that appear in local news media.

Representative materials that can be procured from the community and the parts of the curriculum in which they would be appropriate are included in the following listings.

READING AND WRITING CENTER

Adding machine tape	Catalogs	File cards
Typewriters	Newspapers	Greeting cards
Carbon paper	Envelopes	Chart paper
Cancelled stamps	Phone books	Junk mail
Movie posters	Post cards	Posterboard
Book jackets	Magazines	Menus
Manuals	Coupons	Joke books
Labels	Photographs	Pictures
Stationery	Type books	Order forms

DRAMATICS AND ROLE PLAY CENTER

Neckties	Dresses	Hats
Shoes	Purses	Draperies
Slippers	Eyeglass frames	Fur pieces
Baskets	Jewelry	Hat boxes
Play money	Belts	Suitcases
Telephones	Capes	Socks
Stuffed toys	Wallets	Party hats
Mirrors	Umbrellas	Feed sacks
Coats	Briefcases	Plastic flowers
Shirts	Dishes	Scarves
Fans	Pans	Vests
Gloves	Utensils	Garment Bags
Bows	Ribbons	

SCIENCE AND MECHANICS CENTER

Corks	Toys	Atomizers
Flower pots	Balloons	Shoe boxes
Bicycle parts	Seeds	Rubber tubing
Gears	Pipes	Magnets
Pulleys	Eye droppers	Magnifiers
Tools	Switches	Flashlights
Garden tools	Cable	Sea shells
Hardware cloth	Cameras	Springs
Chicken wire	Funnels	Sand
Bell wire	Hardware	Knobs
Screening	Mirrors	Handles
Telephones	Nails	Hinges
Clocks	Screws	Wheels
Pyrex containers	Bolts	Spools
Tin cans	Auto parts	Clotheslines
Kitchen utensils	Glass jars	Garden hoses

Bones
Bleach jugs
Coat hangers
Spindles

Watering cans
Pails
Peat moss
Reels

Lids
Sieves
Hooks

MATHEMATICS CENTER

Acoustical tiles
Travel schedules
Graph paper
Playing cards
Scales
Measuring spoons
Dominoes
Checkers
Golf tees
Poker chips

Calendars
Maps
Adding machines
Newspaper ads
Measuring cups
Trading stamps
Office forms
Bottle caps
Soda straws
Clothespins

Egg cartons
Clocks
Dice
Measuring tapes
Coupons
Recipes
Pegboard
Blocks
License plates
Shoeboxes

ARTS AND CRAFTS CENTER

Aluminum foil
Braid
Burlap
Window screening
Candle stubs
Feathers
Canvas
Cellophane
Corrugated paper
Cotton batting
Decorations
Driftwood
Felt
Styrofoam
Leather
Gift wrapping
Linoleum
Vinyl
Meat trays
Net bags
Yarn
String
Picture frames
Waxed paper
Straw

Wallpaper
Soda straws
Paper sacks
Nuts
Seeds
Tissue tubes
Boxes
Buttons
Beads
Ribbons
Rug scraps
Muffin tins
Paper cups
Juice cans
Paper plates
Paper clips
Baby food jars
Spools
Office items
Rubber scraps
Pipe cleaners
Popsicle sticks
Pictures
Burlap
Leather scraps

Shirtboard
Mesh bags
Fur
Excelsior
Toothpicks
Sawdust
Confetti
Wire
Squeeze bottles
Newsprint
Toweling
Shirts
Berry boxes
Cheesecloth
Coloring books
Cookie cutters
Cornstalks
Cotton swabs
Crayons
Doilies
Shells
Pattern books
Sponges
Grain

MUSIC AND MOVEMENT CENTER

Copper tubing
Bottles
Rubber bands
Brass tubing
Wooden boxes
Gourds
Kitchen utensils
Coconuts

Clay pots
Carpet tubes
Coffee cans
Tin boxes
Dowel rods
Bamboo
Inner tubes

Oatmeal boxes
Ham tins
Canes
Feathers
Metal lids
Pie tins
Tissue streamers

An Annotated Bibliography

The list of writings on the topic of open education is prodigious. Just since 1967 at least 500 articles, research reports, and books have appeared in the popular and the professional press in England and America. In addition many authors have written pieces discussing topics that are related to open education; learning centers, team teaching, individualized instruction, British primary education, multi-age grouping, and media centers are just a few examples of kindred areas of interest.

To provide a brief but comprehensive review of one specific type of literature, the following bibliography includes only major books on "open education." If further information is needed, periodical articles on topics connected with openness can be traced through careful use of the *Education Index* or the *Readers' Guide to Periodical Literature*. *Research in Education* is the best single source of research documentation and reports of actual implementation of open techniques in classrooms. Although it is somewhat dated, *A Bibliography of Open Education* by Roland S. Barth and Charles H. Rathbone, published by the Advisory for Open Education in Cambridge, Massachusetts, represents a fine listing of books, articles, films, and periodicals on openness.

Barth, Roland. *Open Education and the American School.* New York: Agathon Press, 1972. An account of a well-intended but ill-fated attempt to institute open techniques by university personnel in a public school setting. Describes difficulties and successes, and makes apparent the need for close community planning and support, as well as concurrence by faculty and administration.

Blitz, Barbara. *The Open Classroom: Making It Work.* Boston: Allyn and Bacon, 1973. A substantial and methodical treatment of the main aspects of openness, but is general rather than specific.

Bremer, Anne and John. *Open Education: A Beginning.* New York: Holt Rinehart and Winston, 1972. A brief but useful study of openness at work in schools, especially in chapter seven through ten.

Campbell, David. *A Practical Guide to the Open Classroom: From Kindergarten to the University.* Dubuque, Iowa: Kendall Hunt, 1973. Presents some practical ideas for middle graders involved in open learning, and contains good lists of field trip activities and classroom experiences. Also has an annotated bibliography.

Carswell, Evelyn M. and Roubinek, Darrel L. *Open Sesame: A Primer in Open Education.* Santa Monica, California: Goodyear Publishing Company, 1974. An unusual approach, presenting dozens of items ranging from a single brief paragraph to an extended essay. It is basically inspirational in tone, making a strong appeal for humanism in teaching. It is cleverly illustrated with linedrawing cartoons and puppet photographs.

Gingell, Leslie P. *The ABC's of the Open Classroom.* Homewood, Illinois: ETC Publications, 1973. The narrative of a teacher who came to America as an exchange person from England, and settled in Iowa, teaching a group of fourth graders. Consists mainly of examples of learning activities that might be adapted to middle-grades students.

Hassett, Joseph D. and Weisberg, Arline. *Open Education: Alternatives Within Our Tradition.* Englewood Cliffs, New Jersey: Prentice Hall, 1972. A brief personal account of the authors' efforts to incorporate in elementary schools in the Bronx, New York, some of the open techniques. Anecdotal descriptions of their progress are included.

Herzberg, Alvin and Stone, Edward F. *Schools Are for Children: An American Approach to the Open Classroom.* New York: Schocken Books, 1971. A report of an extensive personal survey of open practices in British schools, discussing how different curriculum areas are affected by the change, and answering questions concerning implementation of open methods.

Howes, Virgil. *Informal Teaching in the Open Classroom.* New York: Macmillan Publishing Company, 1974. A practical description of ways to implement openness. This work includes methods of helping children to make their own decisions and techniques of planning the day. Amply illustrated with photographs of actual open sites and illustrations of pupils records and other forms of reporting pupil progress.

Kohl, Herbert. *The Open Classroom: A Practical Guide to a New Way of Teaching.* New York: Vintage Books, 1969. One of the first books to popularize openness in America. Written by one of the leaders in the free school movement, it presents several suggestions on beginning the school year, planning lessons, organizing the classroom, handling discipline problems, and coping with administrators.

Meyers, Lilian and Donald A. *Open Education Reexamined.* Lexington, Massachusetts: D. C. Heath, 1973. A critical analysis of the open movement expressed in seven essays by different authors. Generally supportive of openness, the work raises important questions needing answers, and points out pitfalls, issues, alternatives, and suggested stages for moving from conventional to open instruction.

Nyquist, Ewald B. and Hawes, Gene R. *Open Education: A Sourcebook for Parents and Teachers.* New York: Bantam Books, 1972. Popularizes the open movement with thirty articles by outstanding contributors. It presents a responsible and comprehensive understanding of the background of openness.

Pflum, John and Waterman, Anita H. *Open Education: For Me?* Washington, D.C.: Acropolis Books, 1974. A practical book emphasizing examples of learning activities for middle graders, including about 200 pages of sample materials to be duplicated for classroom use, with photographs and illustrations.

Silberman, Charles ed. *The Open Classroom Reader.* New York: Random House, 1973. Presents a comprehensive collection of seventy-seven articles by outstanding persons in the field and is the best single discussion of the theoretical background of contemporary and historical thinking on openness. In some chapters, the author deals with implementation in actual classroom settings.

Silberman, Melvin L.; Allender, Jerome S. and Yanoff, Jay M. *The Psychology of Open Education: An Inquiry Approach.* Boston: Little, Brown and Company, 1972. An insightful and responsible study of the learning environment and of the principles of teaching that best fit into self-directed instruction. This is an excellent source for teachers in training and for those already in service. It includes practical group activities, individual inquiries, and many excerpts from the best sources in theories of learning. It is substantive but not difficult to read and understand.

Smith, Lee. *Jack Out of the Box: A Practical Guide to the Open Classroom.* West Nyack, New York: Parker Publishers, 1974. Approaches openness mainly from a viewpoint of organization, with emphasis on ungradedness and team teaching. Defines the roles of administrators and teachers, identifies objectives of the open curriculum, and shows how important community support becomes.

Spodek, Bernard and Walberg, Herbert J. *Studies in Open Education.* New York: Agathon Press, 1975. An anthology of insightful articles by scholars discussing the philosophy and the psychology of the open approach. In the latter portion of the book, the authors discuss five major research studies that attempt to classify and describe open education practices.

Stephens, Lillian. *Teacher's Guide to Open Education*. New York: Holt Rinehart and Winston, 1974. A personal explanation of ways to develop open techniques. Based on the author's visit to British schools in 1971.

Taylor, Joy. *Organizing the Open Classroom: A Teacher's Guide to the Integrated Day*. New York: Schocken Books, 1972. A brief description of the open classroom in England, dealing mainly with the structure of the nontraditional day as described in ample personal illustrations.